Photograph by Jay Blakesberg © 2010

Published by Cranky Touring LLC
2020 Union St
San Francisco, CA 94123
Copyright 2011 Jackie Greene all rights reserved

Photograph by Jay Blakesberg
Introduction and Acknowledgments by Jackie Greene
Copyright 2011 all rights reserved

Visit us on the web at jackiegreene.com
Facebook.com/jackie.greene.music

TABLE OF CONTENTS

INTRODUCTION

There are no greater truths than those learned through the miracle of song. All is exposed. A lyric may unearth a knowledge from your soul that you didn't know you had. A melody may strike you down with little warning and then raise you to a revelatory state. Songs are powerful and the truth will out, *even* if the words lie. Recordings attempt to capture this miracle, but in the end, they are simply documents of the past. It's the songs themselves that live and breathe.

Music is perhaps one of the oldest forms of human expression. It is capable of encapsulating the vast richness of the human experience in a single phrase or melody. Those who endeavor to harness this power are called songwriters. It can be a peculiar and even dangerous undertaking where many go unsung and unrewarded. Still, the miracle lives on. The song is the legacy that lives on long after it's author has expired.

It has been my privilege to have been able to make a living practicing the craft that I love for the past decade. This book reflects my journey in songwriting for those ten years. Indeed, it was a mere ten years ago that I first performed a set of my own songs on a tiny stage in a small town coffeehouse. I've traveled great distances since then, but have never forgotten the fundamentals of my mission: to challenge myself and grow as much as I can musically, and in turn, spiritually.

I've made many changes and walked down many roads. Yet, there are still so many more to explore. It amazes me when I think about it. Like many before me, I've made mistakes. I've experienced joyous successes and grave failures. I've sacrificed many things, but I regret nothing. It has all been worth it.

My sincere hope is that in some small way, I've enriched the life of somebody, somewhere. The ultimate goal of a song is to find a connection with another human being. In that respect, we can all be connected through song. In the faceless age of our digital world, it's important to keep these human connections alive and thriving. I believe songs have the power to do precisely that.

It is common belief that songs float around in the air. They live somewhere up in the atmosphere and attach themselves to those who are willing to extend their antennas. They are like birds; smooth and graceful, ever wary of human hands.

If you are fortunate enough to catch the elusive songbird, you must not merely stroke her feathers. You must feed her. You must nourish her. Eventually, you must set her free, so that she may sing proudly for all.

Humbly,
Jackie Greene
February 2011

ACKNOWLEDGMENTS

Throughout the past decade, it has been my honor to play music with some of the world's greatest singers, writers and players. I can think of no greater joy than doing what you love with the people you love. If the real measure of success is in the joy that love produces, then I am a lucky man; living a life of true luxury.

I would like to extend a heartfelt thank you to all the music lovers who have supported me tirelessly over the years. It is because of you that I am able to continue doing what I love.

Additionally, I would like to thank all my friends on the business side for believing in me. I know I can be difficult at times, but your tolerance and guidance has been crucial to my growth. To my core team: Marty DeAnda, Ben Lefever, Jonathan Levine, Joe Atamian, Wendy Hoffine, Marti Schein and Sheila Volpe, I am forever grateful. To my team on the road: Charles Twilling, Joe Caravello, Evan Drath, Chris Modl, Chris McDaniel, Lee Scott, Christian Salisbury, Alex Nelson and Darin Plog, your efforts are the rock upon which we build.

Finally, I would like to dedicate this volume to my band members, past and present: Nathan Dale, Jeremy Plog, Bruce Spencer, Mike Curry, John Hofer, Nick Swimly, Matt McCord, Ben Lefever, Hence Phillips and Zack Bowden. Your love and courage are reflected in every talented note you play. Thank you.

GONE WANDERIN'
THE SONGS OF JACKIE GREENE
2001-2011

1961

He loved her back in 1961
He held her through the night
Till the dark was done
But he's been gone now for several years
Left her nothing but a letter to catch the tears
He might not know it, but she had his son
Back in 1961

She raised the baby and off to school he went
She had help from the neighbors
And loans from the government
She tells herself that she did her best
Throughout all the trials, they had been blessed
But she still longs to have her fun
Like in 1961

He wakes up on a lonely stretch of road
Been driving rigs for a living
Trucking a heavy load
His thoughts drift back to another time
And the woman that he treated so unkind
He wonders about what her life's become
Since 1961

He lays there now, upon his dying bed
Memories of lifetimes in his head
The nurse comes by and she says to him:
"You have a visitor, should I let him in?"
And in walks a face that could only be his son
From 1961

99 WOMEN

I got 99 women and I only need one more
I got 99 women and I only need one more
I got one over here, one over there -
I got one back home, tied up in a chair
I got 99 women and I only need one more

I got a big gold tooth and a brand new Cadillac
I got a big gold tooth and a brand new Cadillac
You can see me straight, you can see me high -
You see me grin as I drive by
I got a big gold tooth and a brand new Cadillac

Oh, baby --- what can I do?
I want you now, and I don't care how
I wanna take you home and do some things to you

I'll tell you anything you want to hear
Honey, I'll tell you lies if it's what you want to hear
I got this money that I need to spend -
Help me spend it, baby be my friend
I'll tell you anything you want to hear

You look so good, I'm a gonna lose my mind
You look so good, I'm a gonna lose my mind
No need to argue, no need to fuss -
Honey, get your shit and get on the bus!
You look so good, I'm a gonna lose my mind

Oh, no, no, no! What can I do?
I want you now, and I don't care how
I wanna take you home and do some things to you

Come with me baby, I'll tell you what I'm gonna do
Come with me baby, I'll tell you what I'm gonna do
I'm gonna roll you over, turn you around -
Do you right side up and up side down
Come with me baby, I'll tell you what I'm gonna do

Oh, no, no, no! Please don't walk away!
Oh, no, no, no! Please don't walk away!
'Cause I wanna turn you out, there will be no truce -
I'm gonna turn you every which way but loose
Oh no baby, please don't walk away

Oh no, no baby! What can I do?
I want you bad, my eyes get hazy
I want you honey and it makes me a little crazy

A FACE AMONG THE CROWD

Seems like it was only yesterday
I was just a boy yearning to run
You always seemed so tall
In your uniform and all
Funny how some things, they never change

Now that I'm a man and I'm fully grown
I stand to face the world all by myself
If what they say is true, that I'm a lot like you
Then I know we're sharing more than just a name

Every time I look into the mirror
I see you standing there
Ever day I realize you're more a part of me
I am but a face among the crowd
And I hope I've made you proud
I hope I'm half the man you thought I'd be

I've been working hard most every night
Singing my songs under the spotlight
Sometimes it get's so rough
I feel I've had enough
But I recall the words you said to me:

"If you can keep your head and carry on*
If you can share your strength with those who need
If you can watch it all cave in
Get up and build again
Why then you'll be a man, I do believe"

Every time I look into the mirror
I see you standing there
Every day I realize you're more a part of me

I am but a face among the crowd
And I hope I've made you proud
I hope I'm half the man you thought I'd be

I remember standing next to you
To see how tall I grew
I remember falling down and scraping up my knees

I am but a face among the crowd
And I hope I've made you proud
I hope I'm half the man you taught me to be

*I wrote this song as a Father's Day gift for my dad. I remember him showing me the poem "If"
by Rudyard Kipling when I was young. This verse was inspired by that poem.

A MOMENT OF TEMPORARY COLOR

The summer birds have flown
Off to find another home
I long to go, but I am uninvited

I am a stranger here
Strangled by my every fear
The thoughts inside my head keep me divided

I can't stand myself
'Cause I feel like someone else
That I don't know

I can't even tell
If I'm sick or if I'm well
I just go

The purpose of my mission was to see the ocean
I have not seen the ocean, or tasted the rain
And if you will not let me land this airplane
My mission will surely be in vain

I will fly someday
Above the melancholy grey
That swallows me

I will dream out loud
Among the color and the clouds
Is where I'll be

Everything we have in life will go away
I am afraid
But I'm not the only one
I will leave the world alone, I cannot stay

I am afraid

But I'm not the only one

*lyrics in italics written by Tim Bluhm from the song "Mission In Vain"

*This song began it's life during my tenure with Phil Lesh and Friends. One night as we per-
formed "Bird Song", I was struck by the awesome beauty of the tune. I was completely inspired.
I kept mumbling to myself that inspiration is like a "moment of temporary color". It comes on
suddenly and can go away just as quickly. Now, I think of this as my personal ode to "Bird Song".
When I got to writing it all down, I kept putting in a snippet of a song called "Mission in Vain"
by the Mother Hips. I think it's particularly interesting because the studio version of "Mission In
Vain" was the first time I'd ever played music with the Mother Hips. Tim Bluhm called and in-
vited me down to the studio to play organ on the song. I was thrilled and honored to be playing
music with one of my favorite bands.

A THING CALLED RAIN

I think I'll quit my job today
Spend the money that I saved
I think I'll build a boat for me
And sail myself across the sea
'Cause every night the sun goes down
And the morning helps me come around
The coffee likes to chase the booze
The booze it likes to chase the blues

I kept your picture in a frame
I kept your heart out on a chain
But hearts don't belong on chains
And pictures don't belong in frames
People come and people go
Foe to friend and friend to foe
And you do just what you're supposed to do
'Cause the clock don't ever stop for you

She thinks she knows me oh so well
For six nights in a cheap motel,
She gave her heart away for free
She gave it all away to me
But I'm needle-dancin' on a pin
Match under my heels again
Not every bird will sing for you
Don't matter how you ask her to

I can't believe the way she acts
She doesn't even know the facts
But ain't that just the way it goes
When you're telling truth in liar's clothes

Born and raised and born again
I can't tell you why or when
But everything will happen twice
Sure as fire, plain as ice

So, it's broken hearts and dusty roads
And somewhere there my soul explodes
With every piece of every day
And everything I meant to say
And where I'll be, no one can tell
I'm fishing in a wishing well
And i'm doing the very best I can
I just hope you'll understand

Now, I seen all the lights that shine
Countless colors in my mind
They climb and swim and spark and glow
And ask me what it is I know
I know a thing called love
A thing called thunder in the sky above
Now, I know a thing called pain
Now, I know a thing called rain

*I remember writing this song down in a notebook while sitting on the porch swing at a friend's house in Sacramento, CA. I had no music for it at the time. I remember repeating the phrasing over and over in my head until I got home to my guitar. The music came out rather quickly then. The original demo I recorded on cassette went missing after a break-in at my apartment.

ABOUT CELL BLOCK #9

Well, I used to be an angel
I guess my wings got torn
For I ain't seen nothing but bad luck and trouble
Ever since that I've been born
Ever since that I've been born

I used to have a best friend
And a girl for to be my bride
I had everything that a man could want
I believed I was satisfied
I believed i was satisfied

But as I came home one evening
The moon was hanging high
I felt something wrong, something must be going on
And a black cat passed me by
A black cat passed me by

So, I peeked on through my keyhole
Now tell me what did I see?
I saw my gal and my best friend
In a bed that belonged to me
A bed that belonged to me

So, I went and grabbed my shotgun
You know how the story goes
Gonna find me on a chain, digging ditches in the rain
And I'll be wearing them county clothes, yes!
Wearing them county clothes

Yes, the jury found me guilty
I heard that gavel sound
And the only friend who would have thrown my bail

Was six feet underground
Six feet underground

Oh, Lord, I'm feeling lowdown
Got nothing to call mine
Gonna spend my days, wasting all away
In cell block # 9, cell block 9

*This song was written in the garage of my mothers house. I had a little stereo that I played old country and bluegrass music on constantly. I was very much into outlaw and prison songs at the time. (The summer of 2002) I suppose some of that rubbed off.

ALICE ON THE ROOFTOP

See the cars down below
How they go, they come and they go
See the fools, work all day
Fade away and they don't even know

It's a shame, it's insane
It's the world that's happening here
And it's hard to maintain
When everything is so insincere

Alice is on the rooftop
Alice is on the rooftop

There's a part in a play
That I swear was meant just for me
It's the part of a sailor
Who's becoming afraid of the sea

Where ya going? Where ya been?
Are you trying so hard to fit in?
What's the point? Fix the joint,
And tomorrow you can tell me again

Alice is on the rooftop
Alice is on the rooftop

The sun don't ever come
Where the rain refuses to fall
And you can't jump the bridge
When there is no bridge at all

Theres a cross in the hand
Of a man who is ready to die

Theres a bird on my window
I believe she's ready to fly

Take your toes from the ledge
Where your arms are open wide
You're so tired, you're so torn
But your heart keeps beating inside

*I remember writing most of this song on a lap steel guitar. I tuned it to an open chord and sang the melody that I had in my head. After awhile, the chord changes became obvious to me and I was able to pick up an acoustic guitar to finish the song.

ALL FALL DOWN

Brandee danced tables to a room full of ties
Hundreds of dollars were stuck to her thighs
When she could stand it no longer she shut her eyes
And said: "We all fall down"

He stood on the corner, his head in his hands
"How did I get here? I don't understand
Nothing I do ever goes like I planned"
Oh we all fall down

In a room full of soldiers, he begged for his clothes
He begged them for mercy, he begged and he froze
They watched as he suffered and wilt like a rose
Oh we all fall down

Love is a word
We all want to speak and be heard
We long to be shown
All that we can't see alone

I followed her blindly, I stood where she stood
Even if I couldn't, I said that I could
Now that she's gone, she's gone for good
Yes we all fall down

It's all in the papers, it's all on TV
Wherever you turn, expect it to be
It will happen to you, it is happening
Yes we all fall down
Yes we all fall down

ALWAYS WASTING TIME

Do me a favor, don't ask me to dance
I don't want the labor and I don't need romance
I just sail my own ship on an ocean of chance
Going wherever it takes me

This might sound funny to you
But I've nothing better to do

I don't mind
Always wasting, wasting my time
Ain't it fine? Always wasting my time

I'll tell you whatever you might want to hear
But don't act surprised when I disappear
Just look for yourself in the deepest mirror
Innocence lost through the pages

It don't matter where I go
I'll be right here, I know

I don't mind
Always wasting, wasting my time
Ain't it fine? Always wasting my time

*This is one of my very early songs that floated around for awhile, but never got properly recorded. I think we may have rehearsed it and even made a demo for it when I was with Phil Lesh and Friends, but I can't recall for certain.

ANGEL & PISTOL

When the sun woke up too early, I knew something was wrong
They found her body bare beneath the pines
I rolled out of bed not knowing she was gone
Like I had before so many times

Suddenly from nowhere, I knock came at my door
The sheriff held his hat down in his hands
They told me how they found her, my knees did hit the floor
They told me but I did not understand

Angel, angel this life is something I don't understand

They took her body down and someone gave the word
She'd been shot once, right between the eyes
Seven hours later, they finally confirmed:
The case they gave it was suicide

Angel, angel this life is something I don't understand
Angel, angel this life is something I don't understand

How come she never told me?
Why'd she never say?
Would it have made a difference?
Would it have mattered anyway?

The sheriff took me home he said, "Son you get some rest."
I shut my eyes and tried to clear my head
But I reached over the pillow and found the letter that she left
I opened it and the only thing it said:

Angel, angel this life is something I don't understand
Angel, sweet angel this life is something I don't understand

ANIMAL

My heart is a beating heart
Though it's reckless and abandoned
Do your best to understand it, honey

I do not care for most possessions
But I'm possessed by something other
Than the boring things we buy ourselves with money

No, I do not have to run the race
Beside the men inside this place
Of sharp turns and suburban satisfaction

But baby, don't mistake me for someone who doesn't ache
I'm the same as you
With a different reaction

I was born an animal
Wild, wild animal
I was born an animal
Animal

My path is an endless path
It's a long look in the mirror
Never do I near my destination

For out here among the strange encounters
I've counted on my hands to fight and stand
The trials and tribulations

But baby, don't take my words as cruel or cheap
I've got a gentle soul deep beneath the bricks and iron
That I haul myself around in

Yeah, I'm out here trying to do my best
To stay alive among the rapids and the lies
That many men have drowned in

I was born an animal
Wild, wild animal
I was born an animal
Animal

These times are desperate times
We're spotted and surrounded
The hounds and vultures lean and unforgiving

We walk upon two legs as men
We burn it down just to build again
We will not make a change to how we're living

But I believe a change will come for us and those who demand it
For those who can't stand it
Living wild in the gutter

And on that day the sun will burn like a golden hammer
And we will understand and learn
How to live with each other

I was born an animal
Wild, wild animal
I was born an animal
Animal

*This song began as a rant. A hurried, upset scribbling on binder paper. I initially intended the song to be much faster, but it's shape became apparent once I started working on the music. We used the demo of the song in the master version. In fact, the album version *is* the demo version with a re-done vocal and drum track. The electric guitar parts were played by Jeremy Plog on the demo and were carried over to the final version. We put this small practice amp in the bathroom with a microphone and recorded it straight to my 1" tape machine.

ANOTHER LOVE GONE BAD

Run, run, you make me run
It's not much fun, when I'm trying to keep up
Down, down, you knock me down
I hit the ground, then you sweep me up

I keep coming back to you
Oh, baby like you want me to
Why can't we have what we had?
My guess, it's just another love gone bad
Another love gone bad

How can you be so cruel, act so cool
Rub my nose in dirt?
Why do I even try? I don't know why
I guess I like to get hurt

I keep coming back to you
Oh, baby like you want me to
Why can't we have what we had?
My guess, it's just another love gone bad
Another love gone bad

I got you stuck inside my head
But there's no place you'd want to be instead

I keep coming back to you
Oh, baby like you want me to
Why can't we have what we had?
My guess, it's just another love gone bad
Another love gone bad

BABY'S GOT A MUSTACHE

Well, my baby's got a mustache (baby's got a mustache!)
Said, my baby's got a mustache (baby's got a mustache!)
Baby's got a mustache, long as I am tall

I said: "Why don't ya shave it?" (why don't you shave it?)
"You could even save it!" (you could even save it)
Said: "Why don't you shave it? Save it in a mason jar."

Well, you know I love you baby
But you better listen to what I said
I swear it makes me crazy
Living with a lady
Got more hair on her face than I do on my head!

Baby's got a mustache (baby's got a mustache!)
Baby's got a mustache (baby's got a mustache!)
Baby's got a mustache long as my right arm

Well, you know I love you baby
But you better listen to what I said
I swear it makes me crazy
Living with a lady
Got more hair on her face than I do on my head!

Well, my baby's got a mustache (baby's got a mustache!)
Said, my baby's got a mustache (baby's got a mustache!)
Baby's got a mustache, long as I am tall

*This silly song was written on an old piano during soundcheck for a Skinny Singers show (myself and Tim Bluhm)

BACK TO THE BOTTOM

In the evening she comes to me
With her eyes made out of lead
What she needs, I cannot give it to her
So, I give her what she wants instead

And when she's through with me
I know just where she'll be:
She goes back, back, back to the bottom
She goes back where she's nobody's problem
She goes back, back, back to the bottom

I'm no healer (no doubt about it)
But I know how to ease the pain
All the junkies they heard about it
Come to call on me by name

Oh, I know that it don't seem right
But there's no God in the City of Night
She goes back, back, back to the bottom
She goes back where she's nobody's problem
She goes back, back, back to the bottom

Morning comes on like a sickness
She wakes up where she ain't never been
Now I might be more than just a witness
But I will never be your friend

Tell me, tell me why you're so strung out?
What is it that you can't live without?
She goes back, back, back to the bottom
She goes back, long gone and forgotten
She goes back, back, back to the bottom

BBQ SONG

Hey you...let's have a BBQ
Hey you...let's have a BBQ

I'll bring some beer if you'll bring some charcoal
We'll call up some members of the opposite sex
I'll drink the beer if you light the charcoal
Bake in the sun, get totally wrecked

Hey you...let's have a BBQ
Hey you...let's have a BBQ

I know a girl who likes to pretend that
She's the best friend of whomever's around
So I'll call her up and ask her to come by
If we're in luck, her friends will be in town

Hey you...let's have a BBQ
Hey you...let's have a BBQ

Hey you...let's have a BBQ
The sky is a perfect blue
So, let's have a BBQ

*This song was written and recorded during a drunken summer afternoon. The recording was played publicly one time; as our entrance music to a BBQ and Beer themed concert series in Sacramento, CA

BY THE SIDE OF THE ROAD, DRESSED TO KILL

You just can't trust them pretty girls
They're only here to wreck your world
And make sure you never get to sleep at night

I don't know the reasons why
They all wanna hang you out to dry
You ain't got strength enough left to fight

Oh, but I'm in trouble
Like I know you're bound to be in trouble too
And I know that it won't be long
Before the man you love is loving someone new

I walked up to the river bridge and
Stood myself up on the ledge and
Screamed out to everyone, "Let me be"

I got me a worried mind
Gonna find me a worried kind of girl
Who's lonesome just like me

And I know I'm just one of your poor boys
That you swore you'd never leave behind
And I can see right through you
And I know that you're not my kind

Now, all my money's gone
To someplace that it don't belong
I'm singing the broken-down-poorboy blues

I ain't got nothing to my name
But nothing is my favorite game to play
When there's never anything to lose

Oh, but I'm in trouble
Like I know you're bound to be in trouble too
And I know that it won't be long
Before the man you love is loving someone new

*The title of this song came to me in a dream. I can barely recall the dream, but I remember waking up and hastily scratching some of the lines down on an old napkin.

BLUE SKY

blue sky
it's a bad lie
it's a cheap high
it's a fake cry

it's a small town
with a big frown
and I never want
to hear it again

well, he drank wine
and he drank gin
but most of the time

it drank him
till' he grew thin
and he rocks himself
to sleep again

she was nineteen
she was a prom queen
she had big dreams
wore blue jeans

she had no clue
and a tattoo
yes and who knew
what the future could hold

yes, it's untold
but I never want to hear it again

now there's cheap wine
on a cheap dress
she fought him
but he fought best
such a contest
and I never want
to hear it again

BLUES FOR SHERMAN

Sherman sings about depression
He's going through his drawer looking for a pen
Melancholy must be an obsession
But it's nice to have such an easy friend

Now the TV just kills my imagination
The clock tells me when to take my pills
So tell me, what's the new found desperation?
And I'll put it in a song for all the girls

Well, my pickup don't run like it used to
My clothes been long since out of style
Well, I win one hand but then I'll lose two
I'll be damned if you ever see me smile

Well, this whole town is filled with limitations
And it's hard to make a living day to day
I must have lost my invitation
It don't matter to me 'cause I won't stay

They're gonna put me on a train bound for somewhere
Gonna buy me a bottle for the ride
I'll see you in Heaven when I get there
Yes, I'll see you on the other side

So, God bless them all night diners
Praise to all of the dancing girls
And the shovel on the shoulder of a miner
And my momma who brought me to this world

BREAK MAMA, BREAK

You can break, mama, break
You can break down and cry
You can break, mama, break
You can break down and die
If you don't mind breaking
And your heart can take the aching
You can break, mama, all the time

I know a place we can hide from the weather
I know a place we can make love together
But if your daddy says no, then I guess you can't go
But you can't stay at home forever

You can break, mama, break
You can break down and cry
You can break, mama, break
You can break down and die
If you don't mind breaking
And your heart can take the aching
You can break, mama, all the time

I ain't got nothing but my 2 dollar shoes
Ain't nothing like those rhythm and blues
So take your chances with a man who dances
because you know he can't refuse

You can break, mama, break
You can break down and cry
You can break, mama, break
You can break down and die
If you don't mind breaking
And you're heart can take the aching
You can break, mama, all the time

I hear the band playing just like the wind
I see them saints come marching in
If you forget it then you might regret it
'Cause I won't be back again

You can break, mama, break
You can break down and cry
You can break, mama, break
You can break down and die
If you don't mind breaking
And you're heart can take the aching
You can break, mama, all the time

*This was a song I recorded as a bonus track for the Verve Forecast label for the *American Myth* album. Charlie Sexton produced the session in Austin, Texas. The song itself was already 5 years old by the time it was recorded.

BRIGHT STAR

Oh, what a wonderful feeling in my bones
This feels like Heaven to me
'Cause you made a bright star shine over my head
And now I'm a wandering soul

I can't remember feeling so good
I've been so high for so long
'Cause you made a bright star shine over my head
And now I'm a wandering soul

You made it right
When it all was wrong
You made the feeling
Last all night long

Oh, and I....I wouldn't lie
I wish you could see me now
'Cause you made a bright star shine over my head
And now I'm a wandering soul

You made it right
When it all was wrong
You made the feeling
Last all night long

Oh, what a wonderful feeling in my bones
This feels like Heaven to me
'Cause you made a bright star shine over my head
And now I'm a wandering soul

*This song was written after learning of the passing of Ray Charles, who was one of my earliest influences and remains heavy in my mind and heart. It was recorded by my friend Chris Webster in 2006.

BROKEDOWN EMOTION

Bright city lights
Yellow, blue and white
I'll sing for you tonight
If you want me to

I tried to come in style
But It's one long crooked mile
You know I get so tired
Of these things I do

Blue, blue, Honolulu
Grey, grey, Santa Fe
New York City morning
Makes me feel a certain kind of way

Broke-down emotion
Broke-down emotion
Broke-down emotion
Broke-down

"Shine, you dying star"
Sang the strings on my guitar
And echoed from a far
And distant time

I've never had a lover
That could conquer me
But I'm longing for another
Either way, there's bound to be a

Broke-down emotion
Broke-down emotion
Broke-down emotion

Broke-down
I can't tell where I'm going
I can't tell if it's even worth knowing

Broke-down emotion
Broke-down emotion
Broke-down emotion
Broke-down, yeah broke-down

CALL ME, CORINNA

Call me, Corinna
Call me on your telephone
I don't really need ya
I just don't want to be alone
No, no, no

Plant me a garden
Grow me from the palm of your hand
You'll beg my pardon
I would run to you but I can't even stand
No, no, no

Isn't it a shame that I should suffer?
Isn't it a crime that I could cry?
You know that I never got your number
And like a fool I never even tried

Call me, Corinna
Call me on your telephone
I don't really need ya
I just don't want to be alone
No, no, no

Pick me a flower
Find me one that doesn't complain
My tongue is sour
And I know that I might never be the same
No, no, no

Isn't it a shame that I should suffer?
Isn't it a crime that I could cry?
You know that I never got your number
And like a fool I never even tried

CAPTAIN'S DAUGHTER

I could sleep here on the stairs
Who would notice? Who would care?
I could sink in deep water
For the love of the captain's daughter

Fly me, fly me to the moon
Get me out this spinning circus room
You know my blood is getting hotter
For the love of the captain's daughter

I'm still but two years before the mast
I don't know if I'm gonna last
But her love keeps me alive, it wants me to survive
The long, lonely nights out at sea...

I could sleep here on the quarter deck stair
Who would notice? Who would care?
I could slip down to Davy Jones' locker
For the love of the captain's daughter

CAROLINE

My days are short, my nights are long
And all I want is to be home with you
Ah, Caroline

Everybody knows my name
But everybody looks the same to me
Ah, Caroline

I think about you all the time
Your face forever in my mind
Even though you're more behind
Every mile that I go

And I know, when I'm through
I'll come back to you
And I hope that you will
Come back to me too

Knoxville, Natchez, New Orleans
Somehow got the best of me
Ah, Caroline

You should have seen me in the fall
Crazy with the boys and all
Ah, Caroline

I wish that I could say I'm well
But I'm stranded in some cheap motel
In a town that's too damn hard to tell
Should I stay or should I go?

And I know, when I'm through
I'll be back to you

And I know that you will
Come back to me too

Now I see women time to time
They don't really ease my mind at all

Ah, Caroline
So many hearts a-running free
Not a one feels right for me
Ah, Caroline

I might be right, I might be wrong
But I can't un-dream a dream this strong
So I do my best to get along
And go where they say go

And I know, when I'm through
I'll be back to you
And I know that you will
Come back to me too

CLOSER TO YOU

You can listen to the money
You can listen to your friends
But if you listen to your heartbeat
You might never go home again
You got 1000 miles, and 10,000 more to go
You got blood on the wheel and you feel
Like everything's out of control

Well maybe I'm just the foolish kind
Keeping records of what I've left behind
Yet, I find there ain't nothing I can do
I'm getting closer to you

Closer and closer to you

There's trouble down here
There's trouble down there
But everyday that goes by
I swear it's harder and harder to care
I fight the good fight I do the best I can
But man sometimes its impossible to
Stand where you think you should stand

So hey mister give me something strong
Sometimes I feel so good and then that feelings gone
But it wont be long before ill be coming through
I'm getting closer to you

Closer and closer to you

Some people say "never!"
Some people say "now!"
Some people get together and do

What some people don't allow
Some people like to laugh at the people who cry
And my how everybody wants to go to Heaven
But nobody's ready to die

Now never mind my state of mind
Neon signs across the borderline
Closing time and I think its time I flew

I'm getting closer to you
Closer and closer to you
Closer and closer to you

*I hazily recall writing the verses to this song during a bus ride from Alexandria, VA to New Orleans, LA. I was out on a solo tour opening for the great Susan Tedeschi. I remember being in my bunk and having no light to write by, so I scribbled out verse in the dark and waited until morning to see if I could decipher it. I think the verses that stuck we're the ones that were the most legible.

COLD BLACK DEVIL / 14 MILES

Hey, poor mama,
What say you?
What say you this day?
Hey, poor mama,
Where's your baby?
Lost and gone away

She went walking
No goodbye
She went wandering astray
Hey, poor mama
What say you
What say you today?

Cold black devil
Left us crying
Left us crying in shame
No such Heaven
Heaven gone now
Can't go on this way

Listen to me
Oh, listen good
Oh, you listen good
Find a good man
Strong and able
Am I understood?

Hey, poor mama
what say you?
what say you today?
Hey, poor mama
Where's your baby

Lost and gone away?

Dig for silver
Dig for gold
Dig for diamonds too
All that digging
You'll get old
It will bury you

Well, I'll walk for 14 miles
I walk for 14 miles
I walk for 14 more

And I'll run for 14 miles
I run for 14 miles
I run for 14 more

*Originally, this song was written specifically for a close friend who needed a dark and dirty blues song to put in his student film at UC Davis. The original title was "14 Miles". Like many of the songs on the *American Myth* album, this one was recorded with a live vocal, direct to tape. The album lyrics differ slightly because of this.

CRY YOURSELF DRY

Many a month has come and has gone
Since I've been at home by your side
And many full moon, I've seen through the window
Of the train I've been destined to ride

So cry, cry, cry yourself dry
You're standing out in the rain
And my, my the time passes by
And I know that I'll see you again

I long for your touch, your sweet lips on mine
Your love that money can't buy
And I've seen your face on the darkest of nights
And honey, it lights up the sky

So cry, cry, cry yourself dry
You're standing out in the rain
And my, my the time passes by
And I know that I'll see you again

Don't leave the light on, for I could be awhile
There's nothing that I can do
But it's the same old train that took me away
Will bring me back home to you

So cry, cry, cry yourself dry
You're standing out in the rain
And my, my the time passes by
And I know that I'll see you again

CUCKOO BIRD

Sweet, sweet little cuckoo bird
Can't find your nest in this crazy world
You're gonna need somebody
Need somebody soon
I'm gonna need somebody
Need somebody too

My, oh my, how you fly so high!
Higher than the fire on the fourth of July
Look how far
Look how far you flew
Don't let your little wings give up on you

I know sometimes you think you're gonna fly forever
But the one thing you don't count on
Is the nasty change in the weather

Sweet, sweet little cuckoo bird
Can't find your nest in this crazy world
You're gonna need somebody
Need somebody soon
I'm gonna need somebody
Need somebody too

DON'T GO

Don't go, baby
How can I convince you, my love?
I wanted to leave a note by your door
But I guess you don't live there anymore

I've never known somebody that I could talk to
Never met someone that could hurt me like you
There ain't nobody, nobody except you
Nobody else will do

Don't go, baby
How can I convince you, my love?
I wanted to leave a note by your door
But I guess you don't live there anymore

I had no good reason to doubt you
Now, I realize I can't live without you
I wish I could take back all the things that I said
I'd just listen instead

Don't go, baby
How can I convince you, my love?
I wanted to leave a note by your door
But I guess you don't live there anymore

*This song was recorded on a cassette player and eventually released publicly as a bonus track to the *Giving Up The Ghost* album

DON'T LET THE DEVIL TAKE YOUR MIND

Well, they say don't look for heroes
If you don't care who you find
All roads lead to somewhere
And although the horse is blind
There's one thing I can say for sure
You can go through hell, and come out pure
If you just don't let the Devil take your mind

Well, there's no one man among us
Who is safe from the Sirens Call
Temptation's like a crooked finger
Calling for us all
Well, the world's so damp it's beginning to swell
There's a baby crying from the water well
Just don't let the Devil take your mind

Take your mind
Take your mind
The Devil's on your heel, he's close behind
I'm just here to relate to you
Wherever you are, whatever you do
Just don't let the Devil take your mind

Well, the fortune teller whispered in your ear
Don't you remember?
She said, "The night is come, the Devil takes the hind most"
So, get out the door, don't waste no time!
Stay on the path, don't fall behind
And just don't let the Devil take your mind

Take your mind
Take your mind
The Devil's on your heel, he's close behind

Well, I'm just here to relate to you
Wherever you are, whatever you do
Just don't let the Devil take your mind

Well, you don't need to walk on water
You don't need to be a saint
It don't matter who you are
Or even who you ain't
We walk through life and we live and die
We do our best to not ask why
Just don't let the Devil take your mind

*This song was written during a brief period between tours. I remember having a lot of fun making demos for it. The "fortune teller" part was written by my friend Tim Bluhm. This marks the first occasion where we've written together.

DON'T MIND ME, I'M ONLY DYING SLOW

Out from my window, the people are passing on by
I hear them complain but I know that they don't even try
And the lights down on Main Street don't shine like they used to
And I'm thinking of nothing but spending a lifetime with you

You know that I love you, you know that I wait by your door
You know how I'm feeling, so I won't have to feel it no more
But nobody could love you like I can
Honey someday you'll wake up and maybe you'll understand

Now I got a friend of a friend who drives a nice car
And I got acquaintances down at the neighborhood bar
And I got some women, they stop on by my home
But somehow I always wake up each morning alone

And the train that I ride has nothing aside
From the Phantom Conductor with a dog at his side
And the ghost of a weeping, wedding-less bride
Who should have been married but never arrived
And I see through the windows like I see through the lies
Like I see through every useless disguise
That everyone wears, but everyone swears that they don't
Ah, but don't mind me baby, I'm only dying slow

I'm trying so hard just to forget about you
I try not to care about anything that you do
But four in the morning and I can't sleep
The pills ain't working and I can't get no relief

I feel like a hound dog moaning along with the rain
Any day now the jukebox could drive me insane
There's an old man in the corner that nobody knows
He says: "Laugh while you can 'cause someday you'll be wearing my clothes"

But I guess I can't tell you what you don't already know
And I ain't no prophet, my landlord he told me so
But my mind is a burning ring of Saturn flame…
And I feel things inside that I just cant explain

I know that you know how to fake and to take
What you break, what you burn, what you never did learn
Then you turn and you say that you've made a mistake
As your head starts to spin and your heart starts to ache
But all that you make will be all that you get
When the curtain goes down, so don't you forget
That all your regret is a cheap silhouette and that's all…
Ah, but don't mind me baby, I'm only dying slow

I met a gambler who did nothing but lose all day
He had love in his hands but he let her slip away
And all he ever wanted was to give her a win…
But all she ever really wanted was him

*It was during a particularly depressing period of my life when I wrote this. The song came out very quickly. I can recall sitting at my kitchen table in my studio apartment, frantically trying to copy down the words that entered my brain.

DOWNHEARTED

Listen people what I say
I hate to come to you this way
There's something going on in the world today
I don't know what I can say
I'm downhearted
Downhearted

I don't think there can be one blame
You can't point the finger, or speak a name
There's too much at stake, there's too much to lose
It's getting to the end of a burning fuse
I'm downhearted
Downhearted

So tell me, am I out of line?
Am I deaf or am I blind?
Is there any meaningful thing to say?

The blades of war are glistening
But there's nobody listening
To the sound of human voices, hear them make their noise
The machine is too big, better be destroyed
I'm downhearted
Downhearted

This place is crazy, it weighs too much
I'm lost inside the grid, I'm out of touch
Tell me is there anything that I can do

Blue policeman with a silver gun
Shot a Red defender and his only son
Ask somebody and they might say:
"Be straight-laced, white-faced and looked the other way"
I'm downhearted
Downhearted

DOWN IN THE VALLEY WOE

So long, sentimental lady
Is there something that you're trying to say to me?
Cinderella complicated
This ain't how you thought that it would be

So if I die before I wake
It must've been a bad mistake
Depending on the pills you take
Can complicate and devastate
Now estimate your time on earth
Do you recall your place of birth?
Can you tell what it's all worth?
Are you really satisfied?

Paint me a picture of a baby
I wan't to see how lonesome I can be
I don't want no one to save me
And I'm not going to leave here silently

What I've had and what I've lost
Like every coin I've fountain tossed
Every line I thought I crossed
Just cut me when the winter frost
I've paid the cost for rebel dreams
Suitcases and magazines
I can't tell what it all means
I know I ain't alone

If I make it to the city
Do your best and honey pray for me
They say that all the girls are pretty
They say that they don't dance for free

Forks and knives and rusted spoons
Bottomless in basement rooms
Worn out brides and reckless grooms
Are building tombs with pink balloons
Darkness looms an airless night
Just a matchbook and some dynamite
It don't matter who's wrong or right
'Cause they're too tired to care

I can't help it but to ramble
I don't ever stay too long
Daddy warned you not to gamble
He said just pass the chips along

Nursery rhymes and valentines
Blessed be the tie that binds
One thousand mouths can speak one mind
While love is still left undefined
Undermined and misunderstood
She hides beneath her happy hood saying:
"What is God?
What is Good?
And why am I still here?"

*I remember that I was living in Rancho Cordova, CA when I wrote this song. The main verses I came up with while working at my day job. I used the company phone to call my apartment and sing the verses onto my answering machine.

EMILY'S IN HEAVEN

I was half asleep when I heard the news
Sad words on the phone
I just couldn't believe my ears
I couldn't believe she's gone

I tried to make some sense of it
But sense I could not make
How a girl like her could go like that
There must be some mistake

I've known her since forever
As far back as I go
She always had an answer
For the things I didn't know

She never hurt anybody
Never did them wrong
She walked to the tune of life
Teaching everyone the song

Now Emily's in Heaven and I'm awake in bed
Sometimes how I wish the Good Lord took me instead
I guess the good die young and life just isn't fair
Emily's in Heaven, she'll be waiting for me there

Eleven different doctors
But not one had a clue
They rushed her to emergency
But there was nothing that they could do

They said she had a weak heart
And she'd always been that way
I said she must've given

Too much of it away
Now Emily's in Heaven and I'm awake in bed
Sometimes how I wish the Good Lord took me instead
I guess the good die young and life just isn't fair
Emily's in Heaven, she'll be waiting for me there

We laid her down for peaceful sleep
Time was standing still
Everybody said a prayer
On top of Moonlight Hill

I said goodbye with a rose
How she loved them so
Then I turned away, tried not to cry
And did my best to go
Now Emily's in Heaven and I'm awake in bed
Sometimes how I wish the Good Lord took me instead
I guess the good die young and life just isn't fair
Emily's in Heaven, she'll be waiting for me there

*This song was written after learning about the death of an old grade school friend. I hadn't spoken to her in years, but I was struck by her passing. It brought on a wave of memories.

EVERY NOW AND THEN

I've been so many places
I've been around
I've been around

Seen so many smiling faces
Turn into frowns
Turn into frowns

I used to spend all my money
On the things that never last
I always felt like was running
And the time kept running past

Every now and then I get a notion
I start to feel like I did before
I never could bury my emotions
And every now and then
I need you more

Well, I may have made some bad decisions
So have we all
So have we all

But it's never like you envision
Not at all
Not at all

It's hard to get up in the morning
With your head in your hands
I wish I would of had a warning
I might have changed my plans

Every now and then I get a notion

I get to feeling like I felt before
I never could bury my emotions
And every now and then
I want you more

Now I feel I'm getting older
So are you
So are you

The wind outside is feeling colder
I guess I knew
I always knew

Someone give me religion
Before I die
Before I die
There's somewhere my heart may be forgiven
In the sky
Lord, in the sky

Every now and then I get a notion
I start to feel like I did before
I never could bury my emotions
And every now and then
I love you more

And every now and then
I love you more

*I wrote this song specifically for my friend Sal Valentino around 2004. He recorded it some years later.

EVERYTHING TO ME

My baby's got a helpless heart, she's got a thing for mistletoe
The kind of girl it's easy to believe in
I come home on a Saturday night, with not one thing to show
She asks me, "Baby how are you feeling?"

And I tell her, that it ain't easy
To be a man like me
Yes I tell her, she listens, and she stands right by me
Oh, she must mean everything to me

My baby's got the gentle touch, she got the champagne in her soul
She's crazy bout' candlelight and roses
She owns her body and her brain but her heart she can't control
She's everything to me and yes she knows it

And I tell her that it ain't easy
To be a man like me
I tell her, she listens and she loves me tenderly
Oh, she must mean everything to me

My baby's got the misty eyes, she makes love like a hurricane
She tells me that she's true and I don't doubt it
The roof is leaking and the bills ain't paid but still I can't complain
'Cause when I'm with her I don't think about it

And I tell her that it ain't easy
To be a man like me
Yes I tell her, she listens, she loves me honestly
Oh, she must mean everything to me

*This song was written for a girl with whom I wanted to go out with but didn't have the guts to ask.

FAKE LEATHER JACKET

I remember when I was sixteen
I had a fake leather jacket and a stupid dream
Thought I'd be famous, thought I'd be a star
I thought I'd drive around in a muscle car

But I was just a kid, man, I didn't know shit!
Now I'm trying to find a way to cope with it
No words of wisdom would ever save me
'Cause this ain't at all how I thought it'd be

Oh my, look at how you've grown!
Sailing your paper ship into the unknown

I remember when I was twenty one
I seemed to fall in love with damn near anyone
I chased women and they chased me
This went on and on till I turned twenty three

Oh my, look at how you've grown!
Sailing your paper ship into the unknown

I remember just last night
I bought a fake leather jacket 'cause it fit me right!
Changed my perspective in so many ways
And I believe I'll be changing for the rest of my days

Oh my, look at how you've grown!
Sailing your paper ship into the unknown

*This Prince-influenced song was written sometime in early 2007. It was released as a bonus
track for the *Giving Up The Ghost* album

FALLING BACK

You know, the stars came out of disguise
And the rain was hidden by the tears in your eyes
Falling back isn't hard to do
When it's falling back in love with you

You know, the lamp post understands
That you cannot look inside a man
Falling back isn't hard to do
When it's falling back in love with you

I don't mind your wishing games
Long as I can keep from feeling blue
Your momma's rich, I can tell by the way she walks
But I don't care about anything but you

So put your coat on, step outside
The cars gassed up for a midnight ride
Falling back isn't hard to do
When it's falling back in love with you

So I'll light another cigarette
Watch you as you tumble in your sleep
I've known you forever but it feels like we just met
And look here, my heart is yours to keep

You know, the stars came out of disguise
And the rain was hidden by the tears in your eyes
Falling back isn't hard to do
When it's falling back in love with you

FAREWELL, SO LONG, GOODBYE

I stand outside your doorway
Honey, I don't feel a thing
You're always looking for me
And what I don't ever bring

Now I'm gone, but don't you ask me why
It's been too long since I've seen you cry
Farewell, so long, goodbye

I jumped out of your window
I fell onto the ground
I wish you would have told me
That your man was still in town

Now I'm gone, but don't you ask me why
You did me wrong, lie after lie
Farewell, so long, goodbye

Everybody's talking
About the way things ought to be
But there ain't anybody
That makes any sense to me

Now I'm gone, and don't you ask me why
I don't belong, but I don't even try
Farewell, so long, goodbye

FOLLOW THAT MONKEY

Good morning, my good friend
I believe we have a perfect day in store
The sun is shining through the curtains and
I don't think we should be working anymore

We have no obligations to attend to and
no debts that we must pay
Nothing but blue skies ahead
So get up! Get out of that bed and
Start the day!

I am positive
That if we stick together we can do most anything
It's our life to live
We can spend it how we want to, we can

Follow that monkey
Down the alley
Follow that monkey down

I don't know too much about
the reasons people do the things they do
But one thing that I am sure of,
there's no one I've heard of who compares with you

So let us not be beaten by
the hurtful things that selfish people say
Let us be good to one another
Stand up, stick up for each other
every day!

I'm imagining
All the things we can accomplish if we try
This is not a dream
We are here right now so let's go

Follow that monkey
Down the alley
Round the corner
Through the window

Follow that monkey
Down the alley
Follow that monkey down

*I wrote this song as a children's song for one of the many *Curious George* movies. It appeared in 2010.

FOLLOW YOU

Girl, you're just a kid
You can't come around here after what you did

'Cause I...I heard the news
And it ripped my heart from my guts down through my shoes

Don't open your mouth
Don't let a word slip out
I don't want to hear your pointless point of view

Stay right there, no don't you go nowhere
Don't make me get up, don't make me follow you

Girl, there was a time
When crossing you would have never crossed my mind

But pride is at stake
And that's the only thing that I won't let you take

I've got the nerve, you're gonna get what you deserve
I'm tired of being the one you're lying to

Don't you run, you can't outrun a gun
Don't make me get up, don't make me follow you
Oh woman don't make me get up, don't make me follow you

Girl, you made me hate
And when I go to Hell you can meet me at the gate

'Cause I've got plans
You'll need the Devil himself just to save you from my hands

Well I ain't your friend, but I loved you till the end
I know exactly what I have to do

There will be no help, you did this to yourself
Don't make me get up, don't make me follow you
Don't make me get up, don't make me follow you
Oh woman don't you make me get up, don't make me follow you

FREEPORT BOULEVARD

All my good friends live down Freeport Boulevard
Said all my good friends live down Freeport Boulevard
They seem to catch trouble, no matter where they are

Sometimes we drink whisky, sometimes we drink wine
Long as we're drinking, we'll be feeling just fine
Sometimes we drink whisky, sometimes we drink wine
Long as we're drinking, we'll be feeling just fine

They won't send you no flowers, they won't send you no greeting cards
No flowers, no greeting cards
But they'll send your ass down walking
Down Freeport Boulevard

Get on back to your porch swing, get on back to your car
Get on back to your porch swing, get on back to your car
If it ain't a Cadillac, it don't belong on the Boulevard

GEORGIA

I met her down in New Orleans
She was hanging out a bit
Having a drink or two
She bought a round and sat on down
Lit a cigarette
Said: "Boy, have you got a night ahead of you"

Well maybe I was taken
By the fancy way she walked
Maybe it was the perfume in her hair
I think I fell for her and
The southern way she talked
Talked like she didn't have no cares

She said: "Call me Georgia
Call me a bad, bad girl
Call me anything in the whole wide world
But don't you call me baby
'Cause I ain't your girl
Call me Georgia
And honey I'll rock your world"

She got a tattooed rose, she ain't afraid to show
She drinks, she spits she curses
She drives the wrong way down the one way streets

She keeps a whisky bottle by her bed
A pistol in her purse
She can drive a strong man down to his begging knees

She said: "Call me Georgia
Call me a bad, bad girl
Call me anything in the whole wide world

But don't you call me baby
'Cause I ain't your girl
Call me Georgia
And honey I'll rock your world"

I see her around sometimes
She's hanging out a bit
Having a drink or two
She starts that walkin' and that smooth
Southern drawl
Hooks herself a more recent kind of fool

GET IT WHILE YOU CAN

Now I know a girl who likes to mess around
With every guy in every town
She says: "Get it honey, get it while you can"

She's been all over the United States
While I been packing boxes and liftin' crates
She says: "Get it honey, get it while you can"

She's just my type, so I just might
Go and meet with her tonight
She's got a place uptown, a room with a view
Popcorn maker and a stereo too!

She's a real cool chick, and I'm her man -
Well, at least for tonight I am
Get it honey, get it while you can

She's just my type, so I just might
Go and meet with her tonight
She's got a place uptown, a room with a view
Popcorn maker and a stereo too!

She's the best little gal that I know
Always got some place to go
So get it honey, get it while you can

Yeah, I know a girl who gets around
Ain't got no husband to tie her down
Ah get it honey, get it while you can
Yes get it honey, get it while you can
I'm gonna get it honey, get it while I can

GETTIN' BY

The game must be loaded, 'cause I never win
These things never did treat me good
But keep the fire warm, dear and I'll see you again
Lord knows that someday I should

It's a strange old feeling, these passing lane blues
But it's nothing I ain't never felt before.
You nailed down my conscience and you forced me to choose
And my soul I let slip through your door

And I'll be doing just fine, oh fine
No matter how hard I don't try
And if it's raining on the Fourth of July
I believe I'll be gettin' by

The cheaper the ride, the cheaper the thrill
You can't trust the shadow through the curtain
But if I took you for granted, would you send me the bill?
There's one thing that I know for certain:

All I've got is this time on my hands
And time, oh time it's a breakin'
Just one lost memory and the price you demand
I loved you but I could have been mistaken

And I'll be doing just fine, oh fine
No matter how hard I don't try
And if it's raining on the Fourth of July
I believe I'll be gettin' by

Time makes you older or that's what they say
I come to find out it ain't so
Time makes you colder and farther away
And farther and farther you go

And I'll be doing just fine, oh fine
No matter how hard I don't try
And if it's raining on the Fourth of July
I believe I'll be gettin' by

GHOSTS OF PROMISED LANDS

I live alone inside my mind
Everyday is the day I die
I go walking up the street, undetected in the heat
With a thousand different faces passing by

They're out there hanging posters of Jesus
On my block they've covered every wall
But I suppose we can all use a Savior
So I told them to do the whole city and save us all

There's a young kid wailin' mad on the saxophone
And someone screams: "Man, I dig the sound!"
And the girls around the corners make your nights a little warmer
If you just let them take you down
But you got to let them take you down. Right!

There are some men who would lead us to destruction
They deal in dirt and pain and misery
They talk the silver tongue, they got one hand on a gun
And they spit lies at you and me

Most people around here ain't got no money
They got chains that rain straight to drains
They work for somebody who answers to somebody else
And nobody even knows their names
And nobody even knows their names. It's a shame.

So come on, come on, and rise up
Take somebody by the hand
Come on, come on, and rise up
All you ghosts of promised lands

I'm not talking about revolution, no no
I'm not trying to make demands
But I want you to know that wherever you go
You got the whole wide world in your hands
You got the whole wide world in your hands

So come on, come on, and rise up
Take somebody by the hand
Come on, come on, and rise up
All you ghosts of promised lands
Come on
Come on
Come on

*This song was written while living in the Mission district of San Francisco. Initially, I was going to record the whole thing as spoken word. Luckily, I found a way to sing most of it.

GOLD DIGGER

My life's been a mountain
A mountain so steep
I fought my way up from the bottom
Of the river deep

I once had a woman
That I furnished with gold
But that was all that she was after
And when I went broke, her love went cold

Ah, baby your one true love is money
I should have known from the start
That you're a gold digger, baby
And you've got a cold, cold heart

We used to be so happy
What's mine is yours and yours is mine
I'd buy her anything that she wanted
Just to see that little girl shine

Times became different
Smell of poverty in the air
I said honey don't leave me stranded
But she didn't care

Ah, baby your one true love is money
I should have known from the start
That you're a gold digger, baby
And you've got a cold, cold heart

Now I'm back here at the bottom
Can't even get a loan
You must be comfy up in that penthouse --

Mmm...the one that I used to own

They say that everything has a reason
Well, I believe that's true
For I must have done something terribly wrong
To have fallen for you...

Ah, baby your one true love is money
I should have known from the start
That you're a gold digger, baby
And you've got a cold, cold heart

*This is a song that we began to record for the *Giving Up The Ghost* album, but never finished. It was written while living in the Mission in San Francisco.

GONE WANDERIN'

Another day has come and gone
I can't figure what went wrong
Mocking bird is mocking me
She locked me out and lost the key

I've gone wanderin' again
I'm out the door
I'm walking by myself down the street
Like the night before
I should be home in bed
But the notion in my head
Is telling me to ramble on

Every day is just a dream
Stuck inside the Great Machine
You work your job, you spend your pay
But no one hears the prayers you pray

I've gone wanderin' again
I'm out the door
I'm walking by myself down the street
Like the night before
I should be home in bed
But the notion in my head
Is telling me to ramble on

I've seen the sun, I've felt the rain
Busted loose my ball and chain
Seen the Man, and what I've seen
He's just like you, he's just like me

I've gone wanderin' again
I'm out the door
I'm walking by myself down the street
Like the night before
I should be home in bed
But the notion in my head
Is telling me to ramble on

*Perhaps one my most well known tunes, this song was written while I was working at the last legitimate day job I had before I was able to play music full time. It was written down while driving a large delivery van. At the time, I was a flower delivery boy for a florist in Sacramento, CA. I can recall singing the chorus over and over in my mind and writing little bits of the lyrics down on the order tags, (it was the only paper around) while trying to stay on the road. I believe I intended the "Great Machine" as a reference to something I read by Jack Kerouac once. Although I can't really remember for certain. Interestingly enough, it could also have been a reference to the T.V. show Babylon 5, which I watched on occasion as a teenager.

GRACIE

Gracie had a baby, she grew up, she was only seventeen
Something like a stranger, and no one can recall
the way she used to smile

Now, in a one-horse town, no one ever seems to give a damn
But she could feel the fingers pointing
Eyes like knives and needles upon her back

Oh, Grace is gone

Gracie told the taxi: "Take me as far as I can go"
She said: "I'm tired of this town and I'm sure
this town is tired of me."

She bought a one-way ticket with a newborn and a suitcase by her side
There ain't nothing like it
The Kansas City mainline moving down the track

Oh, Grace is gone

Gracie found a job, typing for important businessmen
But sometimes all she could do was stare
Out of the windows at the wildflowers

Gracie cries at night, she looks upon the stars out in the sky
She sings to herself softly
sitting in a bathrobe on her windowsill

Oh, grace is gone

Gracie had a baby, she grew up, she was only seventeen
Something like a stranger, and no one can recall
The way she used to smile

GRINDSTONE

You wake up every morning - every morning is the same
With the coffee and the paper, and the thoughts inside your brain
Nothing's changed

You don't understand how it went so fast
The money you made and the love you thought would last
It all went past

I want something new, something true
Something I do on my own
I need something fine to distract my mind
Get me off of this grindstone

Bitten by birds and poisoned by snakes
You stood with tramps, presidents and fakes
You made mistakes

Every day is nothing but the washed out section
Of the fake front page you pray it's just a dream
And then you scream

I want something new, something true
Something I do on my own
I need something fine to distract my mind
Get me off of this grindstone

Sometimes the scales tip so unfair
Your song of longing dies in the air
You tell yourself that you just don't care
But deep inside it hurts
When nothing works

I want something new, something true
Something I do on my own
I need something fine to distract my mind
Get me off of this grindstone

*This was a song that I carried around for some time. Tim Bluhm was a big help in getting it completed. Originally the song was called "Something New". Tim came up with the "Grindstone" idea, which really tied it all together. The bridge section came to me while fooling around with some classic jazz chord progressions.

GUESS I'LL BE YOUR FOOL

I like the way that you do me, honey,
I like the way you spend all my money
Yes, I'll be, I mean, I guess I'll be your fool.

I like the way that you get around
Been gettin' all over this whole damn town
Yes, I'll be, I mean I guess I'll be your fool.

I know that you know that I know a little
'Bout living and loving, getting caught up in the middle
And I know that you know something
That you might not want me to know.
But it don't matter - it's talk, it's chatter and in the end
I guess I'll be your fool.

I like the way that you can't be true
You're a little bit trashy, and I like that too.
Yes, I'll be, I guess I'll be your fool.

I like the way that you scream and shout
You cuss at me and you kick me out
Yes, I'll be, I guess I'll be your fool

Oh, but I know that you know that I know enough
About men and their money and power and all that stuff,
And I know that you know something
That you might not want me to know,
But who cares about that? It's lard, it's fat -
'Cause in the end, I guess I'll be your fool

Oh I like the way that you use me blind,
I like the way you try to speak your mind
Yes, I'll be, I guess I'll be your fool.

I like the way you take off your clothes
Naked on the john, trying to paint your toes
Yes, I'll be, I guess I'll be your fool.

I know that you know that I know a lot
About lying and cheating and never getting caught
I know that you know something
That you might not want me to know
I don't care, it's neither here nor there
'Cause in the end, you know that I'm your fool.
Oh, yes I am.

GYPSY ROSE

She tells me I'm the poster-boy for American Sadness
And the madness is in the mirror that's a-hangin' on your wall
Cause' if it all ends tomorrow, then the sorrow that you sing about
Will mean a whole lot of nothing when there's no one left at all

She likes to talk religion with nearly every one she meets,
She' discrete as a lover, but she wears outrageous clothes.
She complains about the weather when there's nothing left to complain about;
She says her name is Heather, but I do believe it's Rose

Gypsy Rose, where you going to?
You should know, that I could follow you,
All my life, ain't what it seems to be
Gypsy Rose, part of you is part of me

She can speak in tongues of ancient times, piece of riddle, parts of rhyme.
She seems to be a stranger nearly everywhere she goes
There's no excuse for innocence, she knows too much about it all
She says: "Coincidence is just a land mine that's looking for your toes.."

She lives inside her head, that is, a certain state of mind
Behind the curtain, caught between two walls of faith and destiny
And she doesn't cast a shadow in the early hour afternoon
She's here and there then gone somewhere like the ghost you didn't see

Gypsy Rose, where you going to?
You should know, that I will follow you
Down every road, and everywhere I see
Gypsy Rose, part of you is part of me

She understands her position and the faces on a friend
She's terrified of thunder, she don't like locks or chains

So she keeps a key around her neck, she says it's for protection
For she can open any door she has to when it rains

She stands on every corner in nearly any given town
She drinks life like soda pop and spits into the wind
She's got hair like semolina, seems like it's always burning up
I asked her: "Could you ever love me?" she said: "Um, Well, that depends"

Gypsy Rose, where you going to?
You should know, I'm gonna follow you
What I know, it's everywhere I see
Gypsy Rose, part of you is part of me

She says to me I'm lucky just to be just like I am
But I'll be damned if I don't feel like my soul is about to bleed
She says: "That don't matter none, 'cause we're all lost in the hurricane
Besides, desire ain't nothing more than chasing what you need"

HOLLYWOOD

She's a dream, she's a dream
Getting caught up in the scene
Like a used car bought off of Mister Vaseline
She's a queen, she's a queen
Played like a machine
And all the men pretend that they respect her when they leave
Hollywood

There's a man, there's a man
(At least I think that he's a man)
He's walking down the street with a diamond on his hand
There's the band, hear the band
They're the hottest in the land
Just keeping up their contract for whatever's in demand
Hollywood

Socialite, socialite
Got a fancy appetite
And a thousand dollar habit that she goes to every night
But tonight, yes tonight
Tonight she'll do it right
When they find her dead, she won't be able to deny it
Hollywood

Sometimes I get so God damned sick of these charades
This town is so opaque, I swear the bums are wearing shades
But I know that I'd be lying if I said it ain't a thrill
Just don't come looking for me when the Devil brings the bill

Movie star, movie star in a tiny little car
Doing 90 on the 10 coming home from the bar
Big cigar, big cigar
And a smoking little car
He ran right off the road, he didn't make it very far
Hollywood

See the Freak, See The Freak
He's the flavor of the week
The ratings all went up when they discovered he could speak
So let him speak, yes hear him speak!
His tone is so unique
But by the time commercial hits
You know his fame has reached its peak
Hollywood

Molly would if she could
But she's stuck in Nebraska
I had a truck and so I asked her where she longed to be
"I dunno, you tell me....life looks better on TV"
I said, "You might as well
be living in a plastic factory!"
Hollywood
Hollywood

(Alternate Lyrics)

Now it doesn't really matter what I do or what I say
There's a millionaire buying every hour of the day
If you want to see some change you got to change it from the street
Change it with your hands, change it with your feet

Advertise, advertise
Slick and super size
Buy the car, find true love, and a dozen other lies
Surprise, oh, surprise!
It's what everybody buys
A fairytale fantasy, a demon in disguise
Hollywood

*This song was written in Nashville, TN. I was there for reasons I can't even recall, but what I remember is this: I attended a Buddy Miller concert. I was already a Buddy Miller fan, but I remember being absolutely floored by his performance. I remember vividly that Buddy did a version of Bob Dylan's *With God On Our Side* that was absolutely fantastic. I walked a mile back to the hotel where I was staying and wrote this song. I'm not certain if the two incidents are connected - perhaps the concert simply inspired me to say what was on my mind.

HONEY, I'VE BEEN THINKING ABOUT YOU

Well, I ain't interested in the clothes that you wear
In the car that you drive or the cut of your hair
Honey, you got something that I can't compare
And I've been thinking about you

And I don't really care about the weather outside
And I don't want to talk about national pride
All that I need for to be satisfied is a
Woman who's nothing like me

Love is for fools, yes, a fool such as I
And I can't tell you how and I can't tell you why
Ah, but honey, I just can't deny you at all

Oh, and I don't want to be your two-weekend lover
Your boy-in-the-bag, your one-or-the-other
And I ain't looking for a wife or a mother
But honey, I've been thinking about you

Well, maybe you're wrong and maybe you're right
And maybe we could sit here and argue all night
But maybe you just better turn out the lights
'Cause honey, I've been thinking about you

Honey, I've been thinking about you for awhile
And it's driving me mad, yes, it's cramping my style
And I ain't asking you to walk down the aisle, but I...

Suitcase to staircase, to candlelit room
Where I sift through the silk in the airless perfume
And I'll be loving you baby, I'll be loving you soon
'Cause honey, I've been thinking about you

Now, I don't really care about your hot-blooded sister
I'm sure there's a man for to love her and miss her
I didn't mean nothing, I just happened to kiss her
But, honey, I was thinking about you

I don't really care about your daddy's corvette
Your house in the hills or your pink private jet
Or that ring on your finger you say you regret
'Cause honey, I've been thinking about you

Rat race, to car chase, to trains in the station
Everyone wants to change their location
Everyone wants some new inspiration
But I can't stop thinking about you

I DON'T CARE ABOUT MY BABY

I don't care about my baby, she don't care about me
No, I don't care about my baby, and she don't care about me

Walking down the avenue, seems I'm always running into you
You got nothing for me, you got no words to say
But I guess you never did anyway!
I don't care about my baby, she don't care about me
No, I don't care about my baby, and she don't care about me

There was a time when you cared for me
Honey, there was a time you prepared for me
But those days are gone, yes, they're down the drain
You got to find someone else to call your name!
I don't care about my baby, she don't care about me
No, I don't care about my baby, and she don't care about me

There was a time when you loved me so
Honey, there was a time you wouldn't let me go
Those days are gone and I'm well aware
Those days are gone but I just don't care!
I don't care about my baby, she don't care about me
No, I don't care about my baby, and she don't care about me

Someday soon, and it won't be long
Somebody's gonna hurt you, somebody's gonna do you wrong
And you'll be crying, but don't you come my way
I'll just look at you and laugh and then I'll say:
I don't care about you baby, you don't care about me
No, I don't care about you baby, and you don't care about me

You're just running round!
Running round!

I DON'T LIVE IN A DREAM

I don't live in a dream
I don't live in a dream
I don't live in some land forgotten
I don't live in a dream
I don't live in a dream

I don't live on the moon
Drink martinis in the afternoon
I don't pretend to make the world feel better
I don't live on the moon
I don't live on the moon

I live right here with you
Walk the same earth you do
I don't believe that we're so different
I live right here with you
I live right here with you

Your twisted heart
Is a cruel and wonderful thing
It tears me apart
Hanging on every string
I don't live in a dream

I don't live in a dream
I don't hustle or scheme
I have no faith in politicians
I don't live in a dream

*This song was inspired by hearing the demo for a song by David Hidalgo. The demo would eventually become "Hold On", recorded by his band Los Lobos.

I'LL LET YOU IN

I operate a searchlight
From a tower through a window
Many hours I spend looking for you
Ever since you've been gone

I've been looking for you, baby
Every morning and every evening
You never said the reasons
But you said we'd meet again

And when the stones that you once threw
Get thrown back at you
And you just can't stand to stand in your own skin
I'll let you in

I control the weather
From a dial in the kitchen
Lighting fires from the burner
It's absurd, but it works just fine

I've been thinking about places
I've been to and have loved me
And I've had to been sad to
Had to leave when things got low

So, when the friends that you once knew
Don't remember you
And they tell you that you can't be born again
I'll let you in

I'm nailed to the tail of a whale
At the bottom of an ocean
Any day he'll have to
Come back up for air

Yeah, I'll be waiting for you baby
In the city or in the jungle
Sitting pretty waiting for you
To knock upon my door

And when the words that you once used
Leave your head confused
And you don't think that you'll ever love again
I'll let you in
I'll let you in
I'll let you in
I'll let you in

I'M SO GONE

I'm not going to be civil
I'm not gonna watch my tongue or what I say
I'm gonna dance with the devil
Gonna shovel out dirt for a stiff and shallow grave

I'm so gone
Such a long, long way from home
I'm holding out for something I can feel
I'm so lost
Such a long, long way to cross
I'm holding out for something I can feel
I can feel

Hey, did you hear about Vegas?
She got mouths to feed and only one hole keeps them fed
Hey, it's starting to plague us
And it won't be long before one of us is dead

I'm so gone
Such a long, long way from home
I'm holding out for something I can feel
I'm so lost
Such a long, long way to cross
I'm holding out for something I can feel
I can feel

Now, you say nothing is sacred
You just do what you do to survive
Show me something that's naked
I'll show you something that's alive

I'm so gone

Such a long, long way from home

I'm holding out for something I can feel

I'm so lost

Such a long, long way to cross

I'm holding out for something I can feel

I can feel

*The majority of this song was written in a hotel room in Denver, CO. I was out on the road with Los Lobos for a few dates. I wasn't performing however. I was just hanging around with Steve Berlin. (who would later produce a couple of my records) Interesting note: That particular show, Los Lobos had the ingenious idea to bring along their favorite hot-dog vendor from East Los Angeles. The vendor set up in the dressing room and was feeding us all night. Best catering idea I've ever encountered!

INFINITY BLUES

Got no time for infinity
Yet, there's always a staircase to climb
All my logic is bending
My eyes are two blinks from being blind
If you're not hard to obtain
Then why are you so hard to find?

The room is spinning cycles
A long arm couldn't reach the door
I'm halfway paralyzed
Sitting silent on an open floor
How come when you ignore me
It only makes me want you more?

All I see are silhouettes
Of people that I used to know
They speak to me in confidence
Trying not to let their skeletons show
If the world is so big
How come there's no place to go?

They say that New York City
Is the loneliest town there is
I do not disagree, but
Still, I'm a lonely kid
I don't remember where it was but
I still know where it is

*I wrote this song in 2005 while on an extended stay in New York City. I was staying in a little studio apartment in the East Village. I remember catching a nasty cold and taking too much cough medicine. The song appears on the Skinny Singers album.

I'VE COME UNDONE

I've nearly come undone
Because I know there is something better
I done had my fun and I know
That I'll forget her

Maybe I was young
Too young, too young for promises
The wedding bells have rung
But I ain't so proud of what I did, oh no

I'm going to be moving on
Turn on the radio
And your wind keeps blowing on
Woah!

I ain't ashamed to say
That I loved you the best I could
I think it's safe to say
That I must be misunderstood

It's a lonesome song
My heart, my heart is filled with greed
Tell my boy I was wrong
But my daddy did the same old thing to me

I'm going to be moving on
Turn on the radio
And your wind keeps blowing on
Woah!

The things I used to do
I just can't do them no more
The things I could forget

Are now the things I can't ignore
There's something on my mind
These thoughts, these thoughts, I cannot kill
I keep the past behind
But my feet can't stand to be standing still

I'm going to be moving on
Turn on the radio
And your wind keeps blowing on
And on and on!
Woah!

JEALOUS MAN

Do you feel under pressure?
Do you feel insecure?
How can I survive, when you eat me alive
How can I be sure?

I don't know where you're going
I don't know where you've been
But I have no doubt that when you let me out
You're letting someone else in

I can't believe you, woman
You're making me a jealous man
I can't believe you, woman
You're hurting me the best you can

How many men will you ruin?
How many hearts do you need to collect?
Before all the hounds come to bow down
Just to show you respect

How many times I gotta tell you?
You're making me treat you like a child
You don't change your ways, honey, one of these days
Gonna be your funeral, my trial*

I can't believe you, woman
You're making me a jealous man
I can't believe you, woman
You're hurting me the best you can

*"Your Funeral, My Trial" is a classic blues song by the great Sonny Boy Williamson. It's also the title of a Nick Cave and The Bad Seeds album.

JUDGEMENT DAY

The poor man's soul is a diamond made of coal
He's trying every day to survive
He makes his way, through the night and through the day
Saying: "Don't it feel so good to be alive?"

Ah, but I don't want to end up like him!
For he's down on his knees every hour to pray
Saying: "Lord, I been so good, just like I knew I should
So won't you free me on my Judgement Day?"

She speaks good French sitting pretty on the bench
But I know she's only after his gold
She looks so fine, it's naturally a crime
But she complains that she's getting too old

So she tells her mama, that she's falling in love
With a rich man who can take her far away
But the Wheel of Time, make her change her mind
The hour on her Judgement Day

Now, that girl of mine, she ain't the gentle kind
All she do is fuss, cuss and moan
Well, I tried so hard, but it ain't in the cards
So, I'll be leaving her alone

And if I'm right mama, you'll have to sing to me
But if I'm wrong then I won't be in your way
And if I find myself at the mercy of the law
Won't you free me on my Judgement Day?

JUST AS WELL

There must be something wrong with me
There must be something happening that I don't even see
What's it gonna be?
Ah, it's just as well

I can't believe the state I'm in
I think I think too much and now my thoughts are getting thin
Where should I begin?
Ah, it's just as well

All I wanted from you:
Love me like you wanted
I can't keep your heart if your heart can't be kept satisfied

I like to watch the sun go down
I like to watch her sinking from the other side of town
It's sad to know you're not around
Ah, it's just as well

All I wanted from you:
Love me like you wanted
I can't keep your heart if your heart can't be kept satisfied

Even if the walls come down
They crumble down on me
I can find my own way out
I can set my self free

So tell me sister what's the use?
I'm nothing but a singer got my head up in a noose
Somebody cut me loose
Ah, it's just as well

Romeo and Juliet
Were made for one another way before they even met
Such a face I can't forget
Ah, it's just as well

All I wanted from you:
Love me like you wanted
I can't keep your heart if your heart can't be kept satisfied

All I wanted from you:
Love me like you wanted
I can't break your heart if your heart can't be kept satisfied
Heart can't be kept satisfied

*I remember writing this song at my place in Sacramento. I had just got a new puppy named Charlie. I would hum the melody to her and follow her around as she was exploring her new home. I remember singing nonsense lines to her like: "Charlie girl, you're such a snoop, you sneak into my closet looking for a place to poop." (This was before she was housebroken)

LIKE A BALL AND CHAIN

Well, she...
She's so alive
She's self-survived
She's so alive

And I...
I'm just her toy
I'm overjoyed
To be her toy

She was standing on the corner
Looking like a foreigner
So I tried to warn her
Said: "Watch out for the businessmen!"

But she shook her head
My face got red
As she turned and said:
"You'd better find another friend"

So how can I compete?
This town holds her down
By her reckless feet

Like a ball and chain, a ball and chain
She's in my veins, man, she's in my veins
I ain't the same since I learned her name
She's like a ball and chain

Now I...
I looked around
It's a crazy town
If you look around

But she...
She loves the sound
Of this crazy town
She loves the sound

I was at the wheel of
An automobile
When I thought that I could steal
Her away for a Sunday drive

But she told me: "No!"
Said she didn't want to go
My heart sank low and
I felt like a fool inside

So, how can I persuade?
I was born too soft
To be in love this way

Like a ball and chain, a ball and chain
She's in my veins, man, she's in my veins
I ain't the same since I learned her name
She's like a ball and chain

A ball and chain, ball and chain
I can't tame her wicked games
I ain't the same since I learned her name
She's like a ball and chain

*I remember writing this song on an old toy Casio keyboard. It had a built-in beat machine that I loved the sound of. I sat on my couch for hours toying with the different sounds and rhythms included on the keyboard. Much joy and creativity can be found in simple, limited tools.

LOVE IS A SHINING CATASTROPHE

Locked out on freak-out street
Bags of bad luck at my feet
The colors of 2:00 AM
Leave no clue as to where I am
But that's all right

Rainmaker make me cry
I can't believe my eyes are dry
I had two loves to my name
But they met aboard a train
And they quit me
They both quit me

Guess there's no use to fight it
Lovers do come and become divided
It's God's honest truth
We are all his proof:
That love is a shining catastrophe

The universe just brings me down
I can't relate to those around
Between a pistol and a kiss
Is the space where I exist
In my own world

I'm innocent so let me go
I did my best to let you know
That the rags of Father Time
Are one small step behind
Better move!
You'd better move

Guess there's no use to fight it
Lovers do come and become divided
That is the truth
For I am living proof:
That love is a shining catastrophe
That love is a shining catastrophe

*This entire song was written in order to accompany the line, *"locked out on freak-out street"*. I was carrying that line in my mind for several months, with nothing else. I really loved the line and I needed an excuse to use it.

LOVE ME JUST A LITTLE, I'M DOWN HERE ON MY KNEES

Here comes Sunday morning and we're stuck in Bowling Green
Another postcard from a tired town
Everybody's hungry and we're short on gasoline
Nothing here but empty sky for miles around

Since it gets this way
I guess I must have made an awful mess
I wish you best when all the rest goes wrong

You never said you loved me, but I can read it in your eyes
You can't hide yourself no matter how you try
I'm sick of all this wanting, and I'm trying to realize
How something so good could just come and pass you by

I can't forget the things we said
Or nail them neath the coffin lid
My arms are lead, my soul is ready for you

So, love me just a little baby
I'm here on my knees
My heart plays like a fiddle, baby
All you do is tease
I'm begging please
I'm begging please
I'm begging please

I know sometimes it feels like we never can agree
I know sometimes I feel so far away
But I don't believe in nothing that don't believe in me
I don't believe you hear me when I say:

That someday you'll be sad like me
Picked and tricked and had like me
Someday you'll be calling out my name

So, love me just a little baby
I'm here on my knees
My heart plays like a fiddle, baby
All you do is tease
I'm begging please
I'm begging please
I'm begging please
Please

*This song was a demo that was released on the *Dig Years* album. I remember writing the verses to it while sitting in the back of the band van, traveling through the South.

LOVE SONG, 2 AM

Maybe its the way she lets her hair down on a Sunday afternoon
Maybe its the fact that she's romantically attracted to the moon
Maybe its the perfume that I know she doesn't wear
Maybe its the way she dances when she thinks there ain't nobody there

She loves me in the morning, without warning, before the sun begins to rise
And in the evening, I can tell her feelings just by looking in her eyes
Songbirds in the garden sing to her through frozen holidays
And all my woe and trouble is gonna double when we go our separate ways

Sugar, dandelion, honey, peach - never did too much for me
'Cause I ain't no Casanova and I never tried to be
But something in her smile charms me like a child and then
She turns the thieves and outlaws into nothing less than perfect gentlemen

Well, the moon is in the mountains and the night is making pictures of the sky
And i've got nothing for you, nothing but this simple lullaby
Now, should your mind forget me, regret me, or even do me wrong
You'll always live here in my heart 'cause baby - thats where you belong

*I wrote this song as a present for a girl, but she didn't like it. Tough customer, that one. I think she was upset that I stated we would go our separate ways. I can appreciate that. But I was right!

MARIA, MARIA (IT'S A SIN TO TELL A LIE)

Maria, Maria, it's a sin to tell a lie
Maria, Maria, it's a sin to tell a lie
It's a sin, yes, it's a sin
To pretend, yes, it's a sin
Maria, Maria, it's a sin to tell a lie

Maria, Maria, it's a long, cold road back home
Maria, Maria, I wish I would have known
Well, I wish I would have known
But I thought that you'd be alone
Maria, Maria, it's a long cold road back home

Maria, Maria, don't you think of me?
Maria, Maria, I'm as blind as blind can be
Well, I'm as blind, as blind can be
Because you never cared for me
Maria, Maria, I'm as blind as blind can be

MARIGOLD

So much depends
on first loves and friends
legs for a table
I painted my room
judgments and doom
but I still ain't able
to sleep
Got to sleep
and dream up some dreams I can keep
Oh my, my miracle, marigold

I was walking at dawn
when something turned on
but I couldn't name it
So I went back home
I did it alone
but I couldn't claim it
I tried, yes, I tried
I tried honey, I was denied
Oh my, my miracle, marigold

Everything becomes much more meaningless as time passes by
So I hide in the bedroom with strong curtains drawn
So I can't look the world in the eye

I heard you were well
I heard that you fell
Back on your feet
Well, me, I'm still in fear
I planted her here
right in the street
To sleep, so she sleeps
and dreams with the orphans and freaks

Oh my, my miracle, marigold

Now talk, talk it is cheap
I talk in my sleep,
I know what to say
I say - I said you were wise
to let go of my eyes
and push me away
And run, yes, you run
you run, honey, nothing gets done
Oh my, my miracle, marigold

Now all that I've learned - it must be a chemical change
After all i'm no different from the next twisted talker who's
Taking his lines to the grave

I wasn't myself
There was nobody else
that I couldn't be
Like you - were nobody too
Just somebody who was exactly like me
So sleep, let us sleep
and dream up some dreams we can keep
Oh my, my miracle, marigold

*This song began as a poem to a girlfriend. It took about a year before it was put to music. I can remember slaving over it during my tour as the opening act for the legendary BB King. I remember carrying a piece of paper that I would scribble one or two lines upon each day. There's a line in the beginning about painting my room. My mother recalls (I have no recollection of this) that when I was a little boy, I decided to paint my room in what she calls "very serious colors".

MEDICINE

I don't want your medicine
Sick as I am, sick as I am
I don't need your helping hand
I got a plan, said I got a plan

I like what you did, would you do it again?
What was your name? Tell me your name
I like what you did, would you be my friend?
Do it again, do it again

I don't want your medicine
Creeping around, fucking up my head
I can live my life again
Like I said

I don't want your novocaine
I like the pain, yes I like the pain
Keep my one bad habit on a golden chain
I won't complain, won't hear me complain

There's no one like you, so don't you let me down
You know what I need, you know what I need
But I get sick of you hanging around
Why don't you leave? I want you to leave

I don't want your medicine
Creeping around, fucking up my head
I can live my life again
Like I said

I don't want your medicine
Sick as I am, sick as I am
I don't want your medicine

I like who I am, I like who I am
I don't want your medicine
Medicine, medicine
I don't want your medicine
Medicine, medicine

*The main verse form and melody of this song was written by my dear friend, Tim Bluhm. He called me early one morning and told me he woke from a dream in which I was singing this very song. He sang the first verse into the phone and I loved it. I was astonished that he could retain that much of his dream and I vowed to finish the song and record it.

MEXICAN GIRL

I'm falling in love with a Mexican girl
I'm falling in love with a Mexican girl
And she falls so easily over me
Yes, she falls so easily over me

I'm spending my time with a Mexican girl
I've spent my last dime on that Mexican girl
And she falls so easily over me
Yes, she falls so easily over me

I'm falling in love with a Mexican girl
I can't get enough of that Mexican girl
And she falls so easily over me
Yes, she falls so easily over me

I'm going to my grave with a Mexican girl
I'm going to be saved by that Mexican girl
And she falls so easily over me
Yes, she falls so easily over me

*I remember writing this song very quickly. The phrasing, lyrics and music all came at the same time. I was in a minimalist phase, convinced that "less is more". It's really just a very simple love song. Nothing more, nothing less.

MISS MADELINE (3 WAYS TO LOVE HER)

Madeline's naked, alone on her bed
She's rotting herself to the core
Nobody knows what goes on in her head
Nobody cares anymore
She used to be young; a child of the sun
Now she's searching the floor
And there's one, two, three ways to love her
But one way to get through her door

Madeline's lonely, she's dying of thirst
She's trying her best to be free
She says that she's sure that her soul has been cursed
Maybe just a little like me
She listens to voices, making her choices
Living a life she believes
And there's one, two, three ways to love her
But one way is all that I see

Madeline's makeup is smeared on her face
She looks like she's been burned in a fire
With her switchblade eyes and gun-metal grace,
She walks with her toes to the wire
Well, the world keeps turning, her candles keep burning
Their flickering flame of desire
And there's one, two, three ways to love her
But one way to make you a liar

Madeline's breathing her breath in the air
She circles the block once or twice
The cold winter wind has frozen her hair
But she won't take the advice
And she don't mind the pain, she calls it by name
Let go your virtue, your vice
And there's one, two, three ways to love her
But one way to tumble the dice

Madeline's desperate, she's lost in the crowd
She's somebody nobody would know
She walks with a purpose, so tall and so proud
But I know she's got no place to go
She tried like a train, to get out of the rain
But froze in the ice and the snow
And there's one, two, three ways to love her
But one way is all that I know

MOTORHOME

I looked out my window, what did I see?
Two lean wolves staring back at me
So, I took off down the road alone
In my motorhome

Ain't got no garden in my backyard
But I got a view of the boulevard
I can play music, and I can get stoned
In my motorhome

Forever I'm a-gonna wander
Forever I'm a-gonna roam
And I will sleep like a baby
In my motorhome

Don't let your neighbors bring you down
If you don't like em, you can just leave town
Say: "Adios! Farewell! So Long!"
And start your motorhome

I used to pay the rent on a tiny place
Wasn't long before I needed more space
So I went down and I got the loan
And bought me a motorhome

Forever I'm a-gonna wander
Forever I'm a-gonna roam
And I will sleep like a baby
In my motorhome

*I wrote this song with Levon Helm in mind. Levon is one of my heroes and one of the nicest, most genuine human beings I've ever met. There's nobody like him.

NEVER SATISFIED

Don't just stand there in the doorway
'Cause I hate to see you cry
And don't try to ignore me
Just smile and wave your hand "goodbye"

To you I'll send a dozen roses
From every town that I been in
And as long as leaves ain't falling
You'll know the shape that I been in

On the grey side of the mountain
You can hear my train roll by
Baby, I can be forgiven
But I'm never satisfied

Chase the rain out from your heart, dear
'Cause I know you will survive
If I'm not living by the edge, dear
Then I might not be alive

And in the winter of December
Turn your good side on the chill
But in the meantime, please remember
I loved you then and I love you still

Out my window, leaves are falling
And my train is passing by
Baby, I can be forgiven
But I'm never satisfied

*This is one of the first songs I've ever written. I started writing it around the time I graduated high school. Tom Waits was a big influence on me at the time and on this song in particular.

NOTHING COMES FROM NOTHING

I hear two trains in the distance, I hear two whistles blow
One has got my baby, the other I don't know

I sit here dumb! Oh, I thought you knew
I swear that nothing comes from nothing
And that's all I'll get from you

I asked that old conductor, but he just told me lies
He asked me for my ticket, it ain't no big surprise

I sit here dumb! Oh, feeling blue
I swear that nothing comes from nothing
And that's all I'll get from you

So, if you see my baby, tell her I was here
Tell her that I waited. Won't you make it mighty clear

That she's no good. She's low-down and dirty too
Oh, nothing comes from nothing
And that's all I'll get from you

ONE BAD LOVE

I had no intentions of being a fool
Till one bad love up and read me the rules
Now, I sleep like I'm dead, might be a little bit true
Bright sunlight creeping into my room

Everybody falls down
I need somebody to tie my feet to a stone in the ground

One bad love
Worst thing that I can think of
One bad love
Bad, bad love

You start with a secret, then you end in a cell
With one bad love to help keep you well
You never can know somebody until you see him in suffering pain
He's not like you recalled, the man has changed

They tell me that some people will never be saved
Well, I don't believe that. I don't want to...I can't go out that way

One bad love
Worst Hell that I can think of
One bad love
Bad, bad love

How can I stand by you when I can't even stand on my own?
How can I make it when I wake up in the dark all alone?

One bad love
I know there's a Heaven above
One bad love
Bad, bad love

PALE BLUE MONDAY

Well, I let down Virginia
When I told her I was bound for leaving
I told her that the city air
Just ain't worth my breathing
Then I packed my bags and left her on her own
Moving sad and slowly down to San Antone
And I'm never gonna set foot in her house again

I never said I'd leave her
But I never said that I would stay
And I don't mean to deceive her
But she knows it has to be this way
So walk outside and take a ride and don't look back
I'll be far away by Monday, baby, I'll be down the track
And I'm never gonna set foot in her house again

She says it don't come easy
There ain't no luck for free
But there's nothing left around here
But a pale blue Monday morning me

I'm getting on my knees, Lord
Hoping just to speak with you
I'm getting on my knees, Lord
I know that Virginia is too
Oh, but I'd never thought i'd feel this bad about the past
Hearts and souls were never ever built to last
And I'm never gonna step foot in her house again

I'm sitting at the station

Hanging my head down low

Don't want no confrontations

But I don't know which way to go

And I wish to God I'd see her face just one more time

But I got to be moving on and on the line

And I'm never gonna step foot in her house again

PASSIN' ON THE BLUES

She talked about Jesus
But there ain't nobody lying here
She talked about the Man
But there ain't nobody worried here
Then she talked about Love
And how she never sings the blues

She talked about money
But there ain't nobody starving here
She talked about her bloodline
But there ain't nobody dying here
Then she talked about love
And everything's the blues

I know she don't care
About anything but me
'Cause she's already dancing,
Talking about passin' on the blues

She talked about devils
How she should have been a 3rd Street girl
She talked about anything
And everything in the whole wide world

I know she don't care
About anything but me
She's already dancing,
Talking about passin' on the blues

PRAYER FOR SPANISH HARLEM

Hot night, Spanish Harlem
Full moon, sinking low
I was standing at the bottom
Of your blue window

I come from miles just to hold you
It's been so long, baby, how've you been?
Do you remember what I told you
It's still the same it was back then
It's still the same it was back then

And I hope it all comes easy
I hope it all feels right
A dozen different candles
Line your bed tonight
And I hope it's never over
I hope it never ends
But when I go I hope that you
Will want me back again

'Cause this world that's all around us
It's for real, it's not a game
And though hate and greed surrounds us
There's love in my veins

So hush now, do no more talking
My heart is heavy, it's a ragged stone
All I want is you with me walking
Because I can't walk alone
No, I can't walk alone

And I hope that when we go
They take us someplace good

We can all be kings in common neighborhoods
And I hope we live together
The daughter and the son
And I hope they'll take me in
When my work upon this earth is done

Well, I wish you loved in miles
I wish that you would see
How time says love expires
But not me, not me
Not me, not me
Not me

*This song came in two parts and was crafted over several months. The lyric "I wish you loved in miles" was the first part of the song written. Appropriately, I was in a long-distance relationship with a girl who lived in Harlem. After hearing the Elvis Costello version of the Los Lobos song "Matter of Time", I was inspired to finish the song.

REVOLUTION MAN

When the revolution came, I was sleeping
I didn't give a damn, I was a fool
I just watched all on T.V.
Man, how was I to know the rules?

I'm a revolution man
I'm a revolution man
I'm an innocent man
A terrible man

Now, I can't walk down the street without seeing some kind of sign or institution
And after all this time, I thought there'd be something better then mind pollution
I might be losing my religion, might have lose my faith
But deep inside I got respect for the human race
We can be different
We could all use a change

I'm a revolution man
I'm a revolution man
I'm a renaissance man
Yes, I am

When the revolution came, I had mud in my veins
I was naked in the corner
I was alone and I was shamed
Now, I've changed and I'm ready
My heartbeat is steady
I won't never, ever go backwards again

I'm a revolution man
I'm a revolution man
I'm a revolution man
Yes, I am

RISE UP SINGING

I get up in the morning, hear the work bell warning
Shuffle to my nine-to-five
I come home in the evening, I get that feeling
Lord! I start to come alive

Well, I don't care for cool conversation
I don't have the time
All I want is to love my baby
She keeps my soul in line

One of these days, I'm gonna rise up singing with you
One of these days, I'm gonna rise up, yes, it's true

Now I found out about pain and doubt
A long, long time ago
But she cured my blindness with love and kindness
That stays no matter where I go

I've heard people, all the people talking
They just don't understand
There's no good reason to go on explaining
When a woman is in love with her man

One of these days, I'm gonna rise up singing with you
One of these days, I'm gonna rise up, yes, it's true

Baby, don't you leave me
No! I'll never leave you
I want you here by my side
It's all I need to go on living
You keep me satisfied

One of these days, I'm gonna rise up singing with you
One of these days, I'm gonna rise up, yes, it's true

*This song was written to be a duet with a male and female lead.

SAD TO SAY GOODBYE

She was a young girl with a fair heart,
He could tell it was Heaven, by the way she moved
But he ain't nothing but a spare part
Now he ain't broken, but the boy has been bruised

And ain't it funny when you're young, you live forever
But forever ain't never enough time
And ain't it just like that old, lonely feeling
As the train disappears down the line
Time after time, I ask myself, "Why?"
It's always sad to say, "Goodbye"

Now, I know a man who lives in Texas
Makes his living working on cars
He was young and he was restless
Did his fishing in out of town bars

Out on the weekend, he's the one they look at
All the women know him by name
But it don't matter for when the moon meets the morning
The feeling is always the same
Time after time, I ask myself, "Why?"
It's always sad to say, "Goodbye"

Somewhere a mother is drinking
Somewhere a father has lost his good son
Somewhere a sister is thinking
Thinking about what her brother has done

And nobody's perfect, yet they both blame each other

And neither can hold back the tears

Ain't it a shame, to see your boy dressed in numbers?

In numbers for 99 years

Time after time, I ask myself, "Why?"

It's always sad to say, "Goodbye"

*I was staying the night at my girlfriend's apartment when I wrote this song. I remember it being very late at night and she had to work in the morning, so I had to be very quiet. I snuck out of the bedroom and sat at the piano and started writing. By morning, I had the whole thing figured out.

SANTA FE GIRL

There's got to be another one like her
Floating around in this big bad world
I've hoped and I've prayed, let my life slip away
Like the train that took my Santa Fe Girl

Well, I don't mind the roof when it rains,
But all these soldiers are dragging their chains
You see, I'm alive and alone and I'm touched
By the angel that planted her seed in my veins

So, Lord, where is the woman you sent me?
I'd trade all my freedom just to see her again.
Send me a postcard from the hotel she's sleeping in
I'd love her until the Amen
I could love her until the Amen

I wish I was home in her kitchen, her pantry
But I'm hangin' round with Hangover Jim
Under my bed, all the letters remind me
I'll never be now what I never was then

She's a Santa Fe Girl, a giver, a taker
She's living for nothing and wasting her time
She's a lover, a fighter a blue-eyed heartbreaker
She's locked up her heart and she's keeping mine

So, Lord, where is the woman you sent me?
I'd trade all my freedom just to see her again.
Send me a postcard from the hotel she's sleeping in,
I'd love her until the Amen
I could love her until the Amen.

There's got to be another one like her
Floating around in this big bad world
If dreams were like horses and wishes were cab fare
I'd ride them away to my Santa Fe Girl

SEVEN JEALOUS SISTERS

Tell me, baby, tell me, baby
What you want, honey, what you want
Well it's 95 miles between here and Mobile
And I ain't got nothing but time to kill
So, tell me what you want

Don't mistreat me, don't mistreat me
And I won't hurt you, I won't hurt you
You can love me fast you can love me long
You can love me all night or all day long
Just don't mistreat me, honey, don't

I'm gonna move out, I'm gonna move out
Away from here, away from here
Gonna build my house in the mud and sticks
Just me, myself and the Devil in a fix
Gonna move out away from here

Operator, operator
Dial me Jesus! Dial me Jesus!
Now, I been waiting so long, so patiently
I been waiting too long just to be set free
Dial me Jesus, dial Him, now!

Sun is bleeding, sun is bleeding
On my head, on my head
They call me 'boy', they call me 'kid'
But they don't understand a word I said
Sun's bleeding on my head

Take me home, baby, take me home, baby
Let me be your other man
Well, I ain't good looking, and I ain't too bright
But I can keep you busy in the middle of the night
So take me home, baby take me home!

Seven sisters, seven sisters
Are on my mind, they're on my mind
They all live apart, and they don't ever speak
So I can have me one every day of the week
Seven sisters are on my mind

*Bob Dylan had a song called "Obviously 5 Believers" that appeared on his iconic 1966 album, *Blonde on Blonde.* It was a take on the blues standard, "Good Morning, Little Schoolgirl" recorded by Muddy Waters and many others. I always really liked the Dylan song and it clearly became the impetus for this song. Little did I realize, that's exactly how the great blues tradition was passed down through generations. Through the morphing and re-interpreting of songs.

SHAKEN

California is the place to be
But I should warn you
'Bout the things I've seen
You don't fit in, you don't belong
Your so-called friends, will all be gone

Well, I believe the things we say
Keep us deceived
They get in the way
We run around, we move too fast
That's the reason nothing lasts

That's the reason, that's the reason
There can be no mistaking
I want to know why I'm so uncertain
Behind the curtain shaken

Well, I don't want to go out like this
Curse everybody with an angry fist
We take for granted what's in our past
And that's the reason nothing lasts

That's the reason, that's the reason
There can be no mistaking
I want to know why I'm so uncertain
Behind the curtain shaken

Somebody point it out to me
Because I want one more chance to believe

I want to run - go stare into the sun
Watch the bay waves breakin'
The human race awaken
I want to know why I'm so uncertain
Behind the curtain shaken

*This song had many forms during it's creation. Originally, it was written on an acoustic guitar. After spending time with the late Jay Bennett in Chicago, it became re-worked for the piano. Jay was a big help in encouraging me to re-work songs using other instruments. I have fond memories of our time together. This song will forever remind me of the wonderfully brilliant Jay Bennett.

SHAKY GROUND

Too much time is spent on the dead
All the places found a spot to live in his head
Like the bones of a lover on a dying bed
With all the nothings that he never said

Mister motorcycle must've missed his plane
A thousand miles an hour. Piano rain.
It could've been ugly, could've been a shame
She turned him around by calling out his name

When young Prince Charming wrote the book of love
He said the words came from a place above
Yeah, they flew in on the wings of a virgin dove
But nobody knows what he was speaking of

It all goes around
Some break free, some break down
Some get lost, some get found
And though I stand upon shaky ground
I know it all goes around

John The Liar talks endlessly
He's traveled 'cross the world and the seven seas
He makes up places to go and people to be
Sometimes I think that he made up me

Mississippi singers must've said it best:
"There ain't nothing worse than emptiness."
You got an empty bottle in an empty chest
Nothing more, always less

It all goes around
Some break free, some break down
Some get lost, some get found
And though I stand upon shaky ground
I know it all goes around

Wake up, Charlie, there's work to do
The crop is getting thin and the chickens too
Better get moving, while the day is new
I know you got something left in you

It all goes around
Some break free, some break down
Some get lost trying to get found
And though I stand upon shaky ground
I know it all goes

'Round and 'round and 'round and 'round

*This song began as a string of verses that had very little in common with each other. I've always loved songs that are difficult to decode. Tim Bluhm helped me with the chorus lyrics and through some strange magic, they seemed to work along side the verses.

SINGING MY WAY TO THE GRAVE

I'm singing my way to the grave
Singing my way to the grave
When it's all said and done, I'm just but one person
Singing my way to the grave

The dirt from the road hits my eyes
The dirt from the road hits my eyes
A black crow calls out a motherless shout
As the dirt from the road hits my eyes

I'm singing my way to the grave
Singing my way to the grave
The world ain't my home, but her miles I will roam
While I'm singing my way to the grave

Mama, I know you'll be sad
Mama, I know you'll be sad
Just know when I die, I'll be lifting up the sky
Though mama, I know you'll be sad

I'm singing my way to the grave
Singing my way to the grave
The harmonica moans, while the voice in my bones
Is singing its way to the grave

I come from a small western town
I come from a small western town
The locksmith, the barber, the soap sculpture carver
Are all from my small western town

I'm singing my way to the grave
Singing my way to the grave
I won't survive, He don't take you alive

So, I'm singing my way to the grave
No, I won't survive, He don't take you alive
So, I'm singing my way to the grave
Singing my way to the grave
Singing my way to the grave

*This song was originally written for the *Gone Wanderin'* album. For some reason or another, it didn't make the cut. I intended it as a country/gospel song. It eventually was recorded by Tim Bluhm and myself on a Skinny Singers album.

SPOOKY TINA

Spooky Tina Richards
Scared of her own picture
They all want her sister
Not Spooky Tina Richards

Little sister Sandy
Sticks to boys like candy
Johnny, Jeff and Randy
All like sister Sandy

But hey, they don't know her like I know
Spooky Tina takes me where I want to go

Hey there, Spooky Tina
Come on, just let us see ya
Come shake around my tree, you know I like it!

Her father doesn't like me
I think he wants to fight me
We sneak around so quietly
So I don't think he likes me

Her mama is a stewardess
Says that Tina's worthless
Some stupid family contest
And I think her mama's crazy

But hey, they don't know her like I do
Spooky Tina let me run away with you

Hey there, Spooky Tina
Come on, just let us see ya
Come shake around my tree for just a little!

STRANGER IN SAND

I turned on my mind today
Speaking in shades of grey
I followed a man of no expression
I heard what he had to say

I saw the Devil's words
Sung through the beaks of birds
The road was a winding, silent serpent
Sweetest sound I ever heard

Time is moving slowly
Thickening the sand
There must be a cure, it's out here, I'm sure
Does anybody understand?

Time is yours if you want to kill it
Spill it in the sand
You think it's yours 'cause you bought it
But it's slipping from your hand
Life is made of a million moments -
Catch one if you can
You try so hard but you'll never own it
Stranger in the sand

I saw the ragged thief
The rock he was underneath
He spoke to the world of consequences
Clouds cried in disbelief

Who has the right to sing?
Every living thing
There are no words a ghost may tell to
Eliminate your suffering

Time is moving slowly
Thickening the sand
There must be a cure, it's out here, I'm sure
Does anybody understand?

Ah, ah, ah

What do you think about it now?
What do you think about it now?
What do you think about it now?
What do you think about it now?

I turned on my mind today

*This song is sort of a recollection of taking LSD as a teenager. The memories and feelings came on strong after an extended listening of *From The Mars Hotel* by the Grateful Dead. In recent years, Robert Hunter has become one of my favorite lyricists. He set the bar awfully high - most of us are lucky to merely limbo underneath.

SO HARD TO FIND MY WAY

He walks around with his hands in his pockets
Got a picture of his baby on a chain in a locket
He needs her love so bad, but she'll never know
'cause he won't ever tell her

It's so hard to find my way
So hard to find my way
So hard to find my way

Poor Richard, he's got himself a banjo
He's missing four strings, but he ain't even bothered
He says: "Sunshine gonna come my way, look out
kid this might be my lucky day!"

It's so hard to find my way
So hard to find my way
So hard to find my way

Red Robin's been working in the kitchen
Got everything she needs, but everything's a-missing
She grew up with the radio
Tattoo on her hip is to remind her soul

That it's so hard to find my way
So hard to find my way
So hard to find my way

I know a man who's been working for the city
He pays his rent but his life is just a pity
He says: "Nothin's gonna change around here,
I'm the same old man I've been for nearly 20 years!"

It's so hard to find my way
So hard to find my way
So hard to find my way

She turns heads wherever she's a-walking
She never speaks, she lets her body do the talkin'
She's daddy's little baby girl
But she ain't living in daddy's world

It's so hard to find my way
So hard to find my way
So hard to find my way

*This song was one of my first exercises in attempting to tie a handful of seemingly unrelated characters together. Movies do that a lot. They tell the stories of different characters and somehow link them all together. It's a great trick because subconsciously it lets us know that we can all be unified somehow.

SUPERSEDE

Cookie cried for three days, until she couldn't cry no more
She ate the fridge, jumped the bridge and wound up bloated on the shore
The children they all pointed at another painted score
and somebody asked: "Can I take a picture?"

Well, the heat down here is brutal, it's hard to do what's right
The locals shout that you won't burn out if you don't ever shine too bright
and I wish I was in your back pocket or in your bed tonight
I wish that I was loud so you could hear me

But oh, no!
What else must I be?
It's all inside my head, I guess, but it just reminds me

That I need you, honey, I need you
There ain't nobody who could supersede you
We're not such strangers, so honey, I need you right now

Now all the streets are paved with petals, the parade is coming through
It kind of feels like royalty 'cause everyone's in blue
Yellow flowers falling from a window too...
Falling to the feet of such a coward

The mayor is kissing babies, he's almost way too kind
We're filled to the brim with honest men, they're just way too hard to find
So stare into his public eyes and watch his clock unwind
Then find him old and drowning in the deep end

But oh, no!
What else must I see?
It's all inside my head, I guess, but it just reminds me

That I need you, honey, I need you
There ain't nobody who could supersede you
We're not such strangers, so honey, I need you right now

You see, I long for a hickory morning with a waltz and trumpet flare
I'm doing my best to recover from what time cannot repair
And I'm sick of all this solitude and pre-rehearsed despair
My eyes are a hundred miles away from sleeping

Well I wish you'd write a letter, or telephone to me
This place is dark and there ain't a spark of who I used to be
So the sick hearts of the unloved tell the brave souls of the sea:
"We're all closed up, why don't you come back when we're open."

But oh, no!
What else must I be?
It's all inside my head, I guess, but it just reminds me

That I need you, honey, I need you
There ain't nobody who could supersede you
We're not such strangers, so honey, I need you right now

There's a cracked and pale mirror, hanging on my wall
The church bell rings and the choir sings and I can hear it from the hall
Now, you might not believe it, but there was no fire at all
We danced for seven days, wishing for water

So Greta tells the fortunes, they line around the bend
A dollar for your problems, and five to know the end
They come from miles around, just like a pack of howling men
I wonder what she does with all that money

But oh, no!
What else must I be?
It's all inside my head, I guess, but it just reminds me

That I need you, honey, I need you
There ain't nobody who could supersede you
We're not such strangers, so honey, I need you right now

Simple sidewalk painter, says his life is such a bore
Spends his time with a jug of wine and a palette on the floor
He screams: "Heaven take my eyes, 'cause I can't paint no more!"
Honey, sometimes I feel just like his colors

I'm gonna go down to the ocean, I want to fill my boots with sand
so the next time that you see me, I'll be a much more grounded man
So go and do whatever it is you do, and I'll do what I can
and when we meet again, you can try to know me

But oh, no!
What else must I see?
It's all inside my head, I guess, but it just reminds me

That I need you, honey, I need you
There ain't nobody who could supersede you
We're not such strangers, so honey, I need you right now

They call me pessimistic, but it occurred to me
That we were all born crying and dying is never free
But I still can't shake that feeling, that somebody's watching me....
I just thought that I would tell you

*This song began as a story about a man who wakes up in a strange fishing town. He doesn't know how he got there and doesn't know how to escape. I didn't realize how long it was until we started recording it. Initially, we were going to see if we could trim away some verses, but we didn't. We recorded it directly to tape with a live vocal.

SWEET SOMEWHERE BOUND

Well, I've been thinking, yes, I've been thinking
Bout' some women that I know
Some believe me and some deceive me
And some I wish I'd never seen at all

Where will you go now? Where will you go now?
Where will you wander? Where will you roam?
Where will you go when the sun goes sinking?
And the morning brings a new day to be born

I can't tell you no, I can't tell you
Which train I'm riding, which plane I'm on
But I can tell you, yes, I can tell you
I'm standing right where I belong

When I die, Lord, when I die, Lord
Lay me somewhere soft and deep
Tell my babies not to cry, no -
For I ain't gone, I'm just fast asleep

I know a man, Lord, I know a man, Lord
He had no baby, to call his own
He had nothing, but he had everything -
He had the world to call his home

*I wrote this song while sitting in my studio apartment in Sacramento, CA. I remember fooling
around with alternate guitar tunings. I thought I had stumbled upon my own tuning, but soon
realized that it was simply a modified open E tuning.

TAKE ME BACK IN TIME

Oh no, where did the daylight go?
I must be wasted
Lost again
Oh dear, what am I doing here?
I must have spaced it
On a bend
Take me back in time

I long to go, where the lazy river flows
And folks are simple
Satisfied
I want to be, beneath the pepper tree
A girl with dimples
By my side
Take me back in time

Take me back in time
Where the people know how to take it slow –
Slow down their mind
The crickets hum for everyone
And men still worked till the job was done
and we could have our fun on cherry wine

Oh my, what happened to the sky
They're leaving chem-trails
Everywhere
Okay, there goes another day
I missed the details
But I don't care
Take me back in time
Give me back what's mine

TALKIN' MIDTOWN WOMEN

Now Monday morning had me down
by Tuesday evening I'd come around
Friday found me singing on the stage
Well, I don't mind working late
It keeps the beans on my plate
If it weren't for singing, I might be in the cage

Now I got me a basement with a view,
and I can sleep till half past two
Some folks call me lazy, some call me brave
But it don't matter anyway
We do our own things day to day
I just ain't no one else's slave!

And all the while the world turns
with petty talk and lame concerns
and arguments over what you should believe
And all the while the world burns
It's clear as day, but nobody learns
'cause no one wants a cure for this disease

Now I see women everywhere
on the street and on the stair
sometimes it's so hard to keep my cool
Platinum blondes who've gone brunette
(and some who ain't decided yet)
Lord sometimes they make me feel just like a fool!

I know girls with strange tattoos
and I know girls who like their booze
and I know girls who don't do nothing but cry
I know girls with plastic faces
their own picture on their pillowcases

I know girls who live to love and lie
But every time I turn around
another grave is in the ground
They're selling all kinds of crap on my T.V.
And every time I turn around
someone says they think they've found
the answer to some old mystery

Now outside the apartment gates
there's vanity on license plates
and a dozen different kinds of coffee shops
I go walking down that avenue
same as them, same as you
difference is my feet don't ever stop!

Now I know married girls who cheat
they say their lives are incomplete
and I know girls who say they've been betrayed
I know some girls who speak of fate
and they don't ever hesitate
they say: "life is made of moments, being made"

But come midnight, it's all the same
It melts into a picture frame
and suddenly everything's so clear
The night is cool, the moon is tame
But I'm thinking about some crazy dame
it's always these damn women that keep me here!

Wintertime is my favorite time
I get to see old friends of mine
Everybody's running from the cold
But I know someday it'll all be gone
when youth decides to pass me on
and time decides to turn my body old

But I'll always love that cheap perfume
messin' with my afternoons
and all those pretty women passing by
We all sing the same old tune
like the locals in the loud saloon
just doing what we're doing till we die

*This was written with Woody Guthrie and Bob Dylan in mind. I was convinced (foolishly) that the "Talkin' Blues" form would become popular again. It appears on the *Dig Years* album

TELL ME MAMA, TELL ME RIGHT

Tell me, mama, tell me right
Where did you sleep last night?*
Tell me, baby, for I'm about to lose my mind

Tell me, mama, tell me right
Who lights your fire at night?
You've got to tell me, baby, or I'm about to lose my mind

Tell me baby what I want to know
Or you ain't gonna see me no more
You've got to tell me baby where I fit in
Take a look at what your cat dragged in

Tell me, mama, tell me right
Where did you sleep last night
Tell me, baby, for I'm about to lose my mind

Tell me, mama, tell me yes
What you got underneath that dress?
Tell me, baby, or I'm about to lose my mind
Said I'm about to lose my mind

*This line comes from the traditional folk song, "In the Pines", which has been performed under a few different names for over 100 years. Most notably by Leadbelly and Nirvana.

THE BALLAD OF SLEEPY JOHN

Any day now, the sky could fall
I'm not one to complain
But this don't feel like no paradise at all
Down on the corner in the rain

Old Kentucky, he's a friend of mine
He's got them Fayette County blues
Ain't no woman ever keep the man in line
And there ain't no woman he can refuse

I stumbled in with my guitar
Bought a drink behind the bar
Sat in with the band till after 2:00
Then I said...

"Too much whisky make me tumble home
Too much Jesus make me pray
Too much love and Lord, I feel so all alone
But that's alright, mama that's okay"

Sweet Serita, she's behind the bar
She's got the towel in her hand
Lord release her, she's only 24
And she's doing the best that she can

I don't know but I've been told that
Freedom is an open road
I guess it all depends on how you drive
While you're alive

People tell me that I'm the lucky one
But that don't matter much to me
For I ain't nothing but my father's son
And that's all I'm ever going to be

*This song was written about a club called the Blue Lamp in Sacramento, CA. The "Lamp" was the site of many late night jam sessions and singer/songwriter nights. The owner's nickname was "Kentucky" (for being from Kentucky) and he was kind enough to let me sit in with his band quite often. The original working title of the song was "The John Dillinger Blues". I'm not certain what the connection was other than I may have thought the club felt a little like a robber hangout from the 1920s. I changed it to "The Ballad of Sleepy John" after the great blues singer Sleepy John Estes.

THE GAMBLER

He sits at the table
In a room full of tables
Smoke in the air
And juice in his eyes
He lies when he's able
Tall tales, fables and lines

He plays all the horses
Got insider sources
He believes what they tell him
Though they've never been right
So he blames it on forces
Of course, that are out of his sight

As the night melts away
To the promise of day
He's there by the stall
Making a phone call
To a wife that loves him
But does not think of him at all

He says: "I put kids through school
From this old wooden stool
And all that it made me was wise."
He says: "Gamblers and gunslingers
And old country song singers
All got the same kind of eyes."

Bones is the dealer
A stealer - a healer
Brenda's the tender
From noon until nine
The piano ain't tuned

But Luther can play it just fine

Jack's in the corner
With some girl from Kansas
They seem so in love
They're making a scene
Our lives aren't so small
So as long as we're able to dream

But no one survives
The table's alive
It stands to remind us
But never define us
For what we've become
Is the sum of what's left behind us

Too many fools
Have played by the rules
And all they can keep are goodbyes
But gamblers and gunslingers
And old country song singers
All got the same kind of eyes

It's quarter to three
Old news on TV
The weather man says
It's gonna rain for a while
Ah, but what does he know?
Everyone here's in denial

And the jukebox lights up
And Luther pipes up
His song fills the air
But nobody cares
So the gambler hangs up

And moves to the last open chair
When a man gets too old
He learns how to fold
And it's all he can do to survive
Ah, but gamblers and gunslingers
And old country song singers
All got the same kind of eyes

He said: "Gamblers and gunslingers
And old country song singers
All got the same kind of eyes"

*I wrote this song while sitting at a slot machine at the Crystal Bay casino in Nevada. We had just played a concert that evening and I decided to do a little gambling, but I promptly lost all my money. Instead of going back to my hotel room in defeat, I decided to write this song. As I surveyed the room, I noticed one man who seemed beat up and downtrodden. Intent on winning, it seemed as if he never left the table. He became the inspiration for this song.

THE HOLY LAND

The rifles rang
The soldiers came
An awful siren sang
Bodies hang
In broken trees
All the leaves were stained

Yesterday
I heard him say
There is no other way
But there's a price
For paradise
That I am made to pay

How am I to be my brother's keeper
When the knife keeps cutting and the wound gets deeper?
How am I to do what's right?

How am I to hear my babes a callin'?
When the death planes fly and the bombs come falling down
Every night

In the land, in the land
In the land, the Holy Land

I can't ignore
The dogs of war
They scratch upon my door
They take the poor
It's understood
What they use us for

But I have seen
In my dreams
A land of calm serene
So now I pray
There comes a day
When we shall be redeemed

How am I supposed to trust my neighbor
When the blood of my kin is drying on his saber?
How am I supposed to care?

How am I supposed to love somebody?
When the land is bare and the hate comes flooding down
From everywhere

In the land, in the land
In the land, the Holy Land

*I started writing this song while on the road with Phil Lesh and Friends. We had some long
drives, so I was carrying some pretty heavy reading material on the bus. At some point after the
tour, it just spilled out.

THE LORD MISTREATS ME

Well, I woke up this morning
Found a note tied to my bed
Baby's gone and left me,
Oh, that's what it said
Oh yeah! The fire's gone
I swear the Lord mistreats me
And the Devil done did me wrong

It's hot as hell in the summer
But all I feel is rain
She bought herself a ticket
Along down the train
Oh yeah! The fire's gone
I swear the Lord mistreats me
And the Devil done did me wrong

Girls will be girls and
Boys will be boys
I just want to drink a bottle of wine
Go to town and make some noise
Oh yeah! The fire's gone
I swear the Lord mistreats me
And the Devil done did me wrong

THE RED AND THE ROSE

I'm a sinner, and you're a saint
Baby I love your new coat of paint
So I'll keep on singing till these blues turn to gold

I'll test the poison, I'll break the law
Write your name on a highway wall
They say the higher you go, the better you are
But the harder you'll hit when you fall

Baby, I can't go running on empty
You take the red from the rose
All I've got is what you've left me

Now a dollar saved is a dollar lost
Look at what all these feelings cost
I'm down on a dime, I'm wasting my time
And I can't seem to find words I've lost

So ring around the rosy, babe
You might think that you've got it made
But everyone knows, you keep changing your clothes
There's a bill that will never get paid

Baby, I can't go running on empty
You take the red from the rose
Hide that picture man, it always tempts me

THE RUSTY NAIL

Well, I broke my back just for her
I got off track, now that's for sure
I used to give her my money, I'd tell you no lie
It cost me 20 dollars every time she'd cry
But I don't care no more
'cause she ain't mine

And that rusty nail
Gave me a thrill
That rusty nail
Do me like she never will
Well, I know there's another man
That she found
'Cause the only time she's loving
Is when I ain't around and
That nail gonna nail me in the ground

Sometimes it's raining, sometimes it ain't
Sometimes I'm changing, sometimes I can't
Sometimes I'm right, sometimes I'm wrong
Most times I feel like I just don't belong
But the whole time I stay here all night long

And that rusty nail
Kissed me goodnight
Took all my money
Turned out the light
Well, I had a little girl,
But she ain't around
My nerves are scattered and
I come unwound
And that nail gonna nail me in the ground

TILL THE LIGHT COMES

Broke down on a back road
I can't find no cover anywhere I go
I need the comfort of a girl I know
From back in my hometown

One line, mama one kiss
How you gonna stand there?
Don't you do me like this
You got the bullets that don't ever miss
They lay me on the ground

I want to see you in the light
I'm gonna keep you in my sight
Till the light comes

My friends don't know me
They cook me in the fire, give me third degree
I ain't nothing like I used to be
But Lord, I'm sinking down

Swing wide, mama swing low
Come and love me baby, before I have to go
You got the whip and baby, I gotta row
Unless I wanna drown

I want to see you in the light
I'm gonna keep you in my sight
Till the light comes

Oh, and
I want to see you in the light
I'm gonna keep you in my sight
Till the light comes

How can I get closer to you?
What am I to do?
Only thing I asked of you

How can I get closer to you?
What am I to do?
Only thing I asked of you

*I wrote this song while waiting for my flight at the Denver airport. I had a guitar with me, so I started playing it and working it out, totally unaware that people were staring. Somebody got upset and blurted out: "I can't wait till the flight comes." But I misheard him. I thought he said "light." My mistake.

TRAVELIN' SONG

Well, I woke up Wednesday morning with bad weather in my brain,
I lay awake awhile, ignoring all the rain
Now everybody's talkin' about who they plan to be,
Everybody's talkin', everybody except me…

And no one cares about your heartache or which lonely town you're from
You got to take your salvation boy - however it may come
And I can't help but think about what I've done wrong
To deserve this a-roamin' this a-travelin' song

Now I got a little money and I got a little time,
I got myself a pickup truck that I can call mine
I got myself a guitar and I got myself some friends
Some folks say I'm lucky, but I think it all depends…

On the lens that you are looking through and the music that you hear
'Cause sometimes you don't recognize your own face in the mirror
And I can't help but think about what I done wrong
To deserve this a-roamin' this a-travelin' song

Out here on the highway, everything's so slow,
I thought I knew my way home, but now I just don't know
I'm going down the road with all them eastern winds a-blowin'
I'm going down the road and I don't care where it's going…

So one more cup of coffee and the radio is on
And I'll slip out your door to the breaking of dawn
And I can't help but think about what I done wrong
To deserve this a-roamin' this a-travelin' song

UPHILL MOUNTAIN

Big Joe Turner, Elmore James*
Street survivor selling walking canes
Give your babies holy names for me

Now I don't know, but I've been told
You never grow up and you'll never get old
You can watch the world being bought and sold
All on your T.V.

Sometimes it gets a little rough
Like the wheel's made of steel going an uphill mountain
Stand tall if you're gonna stand at all
And if you're gonna fall, well you might as well fall

Build a house honey, make it home
Gonna make a place, man, where I can be alone
Don't the yard look pretty when it's overgrown?
Standing six feet tall

This ain't a right but it's a living
You've got to take just what you are given
'Cause luck only matters with the cards and the women
and sometimes not at all

Sometimes it gets a little rough
Like the wheel's made of steel going an uphill mountain
Stand tall if you're gonna stand at all
And if you're gonna fall, well you might as well fall

Peeping Tom said to Madame Rose
"I've seen you twice already without your clothes,
Now what I suggest honey, what I propose
is that you see me without mine"

Tell John Henry* and Cassius Clay
Swinging iron for a living is one Hell of a way
But whatever you do, don't let your hammer stray
And I believe we'll be just fine

Sometimes it gets a little rough
Like the wheel's made of steel going an uphill mountain
Stand tall if you're gonna stand at all
And if you're gonna crawl, well you might as well crawl

*Big Joe Turner was an iconic blues singer known for his recording of the early rock and roll hit "Shake, Rattle and Roll". Elmore James was an American blues singer and slide guitar player who recorded "The Sky is Crying", popularized by the late Stevie Ray Vaughn. John Henry is a folklore character said to have massive strength and the ability to lift an extra-heavy hammer. When the railroad owners employ a machine to replace the men, John Henry beats the new steam-powered hammer in a contest in order to save the jobs of his fellow workers. He is so exhausted that he dies. John Henry has come to symbolize the plight of the working class and is probably the most common character in American Folk Music.

WAITING FOR THE WHISTLE

She said: "This town is killing me;
all I remember are a thousand faces."
I was blind but now I see
Just give me some time, child, and I'll take you places
Far away from here

She said: "Roses don't mean a thing."
I said: "I'll have to disagree."
She said she don't want no diamond ring
I just want you to be close by me now

And there ain't nothing to explain
We're all just waiting for the whistle to blow
And there ain't no way she's gonna chain my horses
Not when she's waiting for the whistle to blow

She said the scenery is all the same
"I'm sick and tired of this drugstore living."
I said: "It's a low-down dirty shame
you never get back what you're giving."

She said: "I was born to die alone."
I said I'll have to disagree
She said: "There ain't no time to be wrong;
so come inside boy and waste your love
on me."

And there ain't nothing to explain
We're all just waiting for the whistle to blow
And there ain't no way she's gonna chain my horses
Not when she's waiting for the whistle to blow

WHAT I KNOW

Some time ago, it occurred to me
that the only thing that you get for free
is the smile on her face, when your foot
goes through the door

'Cause what it is ain't what it seems
like the promises from magazines
And you say your plate is empty,
but you never ask for more

What I know
I know, just can't save me now
Oh, no

Bless me father, 'cause I'm the one
I got no sword, I got no gun
But when the day is said and done,
I believe I'll still be here

And just because my eyes are down
don't mean that I can't look around
watch them smiles turn to frowns,
the laughs that turn to tears

What I know
I know, just can't save me now
Oh, no

Some folks like to have it all
I see it in my crystal ball
and some folks are just bound to fall
and others born to lose

So you can build your mansion,
you can build your throne
but the more you have, the less you own
and soon your time is come and gone
and then you'll have to choose

What I know
I know, just can't save me now
Oh, no

Electronic men who supervise
and the cell talk and the super-size
has taken me by surprise and
I'm weary to the bone

And sometimes all I seem to see
is the Jukebox of Hypocrisy
Be not what you claim to be,
but you claim to be your own

What I know
I know, just can't save me now
Oh no

You cannot advertise to me
I know you're lying, can't you see
Now, if you'll kindly exit my TV
I'll show you to the door

"Save the coupons, save the cans"
I can't keep up with the demands
Now my babe is washed by dirty hands
and I can't take no more

WHEN YOU RETURN

There's too much work today
And I don't want to do anything today
No I don't want to
But the barn out there needs maintenance
And I ain't got the patience...
I think I'd rather sit and watch it burn
Wait right here baby, till you return

All our friends come by, they annoy me
They try to get me high, but they destroy me
They think they do me service
But they just make me nervous
What goes on ain't nobody's concern
I'll tell you everything when you return

And I can't stand it here
If you're not standing here
I can't keep it together
I can't be brave forever
You know not how a man like me can yearn
I'll keep you by my side when you return

I can't stand it here
If you're not standing here
I wish that I was tougher
But it serves me right to suffer
You know not how a man like me can yearn
I'll tell you everything when you return

There's too much work today, and I don't care to
Do all the things they say, because it's not fair to
Turn this house into a home, it can't be done alone
Give me one more chance that I may earn
Earn back you, baby when you return

*The inspiration for this song was a dream I had about Levon Helm. Long before I ever had the opportunity to meet him, he was in my dream. I can't recall exactly what the dream was about, but I remember waking up and starting to figure out this song.

WHEN YOU'RE WALKING AWAY

Well I ain't gonna ask you what you're doing here
I know you got your reasons, but honey they ain't ever clear
And maybe it's just better that you never stay
I love you more when you're walking away

I ain't gonna ask you what's on your mind
It's hard enough for my own head to unwind
The world is getting smaller each and every day
I love you more when you're walking away

When you're walking away
Baby, I get high like I never could
You don't stay, though sometimes I wish you would
Everything's clear when you're not here...

Lonesome is a candle in the night:
A one-room bedroom window crying light
You take me for granted, but baby thats okay
I love you more when you're walking away

When you're walking away
Baby, I get high like I never could
You don't stay, though sometimes I wish you would
Everything's clear when you're not here...

Well I ain't gonna ask you what you're doing here
Take what you can get and then disappear
Ah but that's alright, mama, you can leave me any day
'Cause I love you more while you're walking away
I love you more when you're walking away
I love you more...

WHERE THE RAIN DON'T GO

You're so demanding
Misunderstanding
Nothing is good enough for you

I tried my best to
Pass all your tests
But I guess I failed those too

Give me your best goodbye
There's fire in the tires
And I wanna go where the rain don't go

You say you want me
But then you haunt me
I've never felt so confused

You tell me lies
Through sacred eyes
How can you act so amused?

Give me your best goodbye
There's fire in the tires
And I wanna go where the rain don't go

Once I was helpless
I could not help this
Feeling I had in my bones

Now I'm invested
My soul's been rested
And I do not feel that alone

Give me your best goodbye
There's fire in the tires
And I wanna go where the rain don't go

And this is my last goodbye
There's fire in the tires
And I wanna go where the rain don't go
Where the rain don't go

*I wrote this song down after seeing the great Lucinda Williams perform at a festival. We had just finished playing on another stage and were fortunate enough to catch her set. I remember writing some of the words down on my hand, since there was no paper around.

WORN OUT WELCOME

I can see by your eyes that you're tired of me
I can see that you're easily swayed
I knew that we'd get here eventually
Our minds have already been made

If I've worn out my welcome
If I'm worn out, you should say
And if I've worn out my welcome, I'm worn out
And I have no more reasons to stay

You gave me shelter, a place to keep warm
You gave me a nail for my hat
Out there it's raining a cold winter storm
But in here it's colder than that

If I've worn out my welcome
If I'm worn out, you should say
'Cause if I've worn out my welcome, I'm worn out
And I have no more reasons to stay

Close tight the window, don't change your plans
Nobody stands in your way
But keep close the memories we made with our hands
'Cause you might want them someday

If I've worn out my welcome
If I'm worn out, you should say
'Cause if I've worn out my welcome, I'm worn out
And I have no more reasons to stay

If I've worn out my welcome, I'm worn out
And I have no more reasons to stay
No, I have no more reasons to stay

WRITE A LETTER HOME

Cigarettes are burning down to my fingers
In my motel, where the smell still lingers
From the night before
With a ten dollar whore who didn't even know my name

The TV says nothing, nothing to me
And I feel so low in the highest degree
Like a tree with no root, like a gun that don't shoot
Like a dog outside on a chain

And theres no use for me to sit here and moan
Many a man has been more alone
But I might feel better if I write a letter...
If I write a letter home

Yeah I heard the news 'bout that old gang of mine
They're all getting married, they're all doing fine
They're all getting older, and needing a shoulder
That's easy to lean on...

But as for me, I'm half way to Denver
How long has it been? I just can't remember
It all starts to fade, 'cause the life that I've made
Is the life that I dream on...

And theres no use for me to sit here and moan
Many a man has been more alone
But I might feel better if I write a letter...
If I write a letter home

Now I can't help but to be who I am
Though I've let many women slip from my hands
I've let them all go. Why? I don't know,
It just made me feel like a man

But what I know now, though it may be too late
You've got to love someone and let go the weight
You've got to make do when you find love that's true
This now I understand...

And there's no use for me to sit here and moan
Many a man has been more alone
But I might feel better if I write a letter...
If I write a letter home
If I write a letter home

*I wrote this song late at night while watching television. I can't remember what was on, but it
was very late and I think it might have been a John Wayne movie. I hit the mute button and
wrote down what I thought the characters on the screen might be saying.

Appendix

DISCOGRAPHY (Studio Records)

Rusty Nails
Originally self-released November 26th, 2001

Pale Blue Monday
Santa Fe Girl
The Lord Mistreats Me
Georgia
Passin' On The Blues
Blue Sky
Gettin' By
The Rusty Nail
Waiting For The Whistle
Falling Back
Never Satisfied
What I Know
Freeport Boulevard

Gone Wanderin'
Dig Music November 19th, 2002

Gone Wanderin'
Tell Me Mama, Tell Me Right
Travelin' Song
Mexican Girl
Down In The Valley Woe
Cry Yourself Dry
By The Side of the Road, Dressed to Kill
Freeport Boulevard
Judgement Day
Gracie
Maria, Maria (It's a Sin to Tell a Lie)
The Ballad of Sleepy John
Messin' With The Kid* (bonus track)

Sweet Somewhere Bound
Dig Music July 20th, 2004
Verve Forecast re-issue 2005

About Cell Block #9
Honey I Been Thinking About You
Sweet Somewhere Bound
A Thing Called Rain
Alice On The Rooftop
Seven Jealous Sisters
Emily's In Heaven
Miss Madeline (3 Ways To Love Her)
I Don't Care About My Baby
Write A Letter Home
Sad To Say Goodbye
Everything To Me
Don't Mind Me, I'm Only Dying Slow

American Myth
Verve Forecast March 14th, 2006

Intro
Hollywood
So Hard To Find My Way
Just As Well
I'm So Gone
Never Satisfied (Revisited)
Love Song, 2 AM
When You're Walking Away
Cold Black Devil/14 Miles
Closer To You
I'll Let You In
Farewell, So Long, Goodbye
Supersede
Marigold

The Dig Years
Dig Music July 24th, 2007

Gone Wanderin'
Travelin' Song
Georgia
Tell Me Mama, Tell Me Right
Sweet Somewhere Bound
Gypsy Rose
Mexican Girl
Love Me Just A Little, I'm Down Here On
   My Knees
The Ballad Of Sleepy John
By The Side Of The Road, Dressed To Kill
Talkin' Midtown Women
The Red And The Rose
The Rusty Nail
Gettin' By
I've Come Undone
Falling Back
Down In The Valley Woe
Worn Out Welcome

Giving Up The Ghost
429 Records April 1st, 2008

Shaken
Animal
I Don't Live In A Dream
Like A Ball And Chain
Uphill Mountain
Don't Let The Devil Take Your Mind
Prayer For Spanish Harlem
Downhearted
Follow You
Another Love Gone Bad
When You Return
Ghosts Of Promised Lands

Small Tempest
Side Pilot July 27th, 2009

Call Me, Corinna
Brokedown Emotion
Caroline
The Gambler
Love Is A Shining Catastrophe

Till The Light Comes
429 Records June 29th, 2010

Shaky Ground
Stranger In Sand
Medicine
Grindstone
A Moment Of Temporary Color
Spooky Tina
1961
Take Me Back In Time
The Holy Land
Till The Light Comes

Bonus Tracks
Bonus tracks appear in various retail and
digital versions of their respective records

Break Mama, Break (American Myth)
Fake Leather Jacket (Giving Up The Ghost)
Don't Go (Giving Up The Ghost)
Back To The Bottom (Till The Light Comes)
Revolution Man (Till The Light Comes)

Other records
Skinny Singers Strike Again! (Skinny Singers)
Every Now And Then (Sal Valentino) -
Contains the song *"Every Now And Then"*
Something In The Water (Chris Webster) -
Contains the song *"Bright Star"*

All songs written by Jackie Greene except:

"Don't Let The Devil Take Your Mind" by Jackie Greene and Tim Bluhm
"Medicine" by Jackie Greene and Tim Bluhm
"Shaky Ground" by Jackie Greene and Tim Bluhm
"Stranger In Sand" by Jackie Greene and Tim Bluhm
"A Moment Of Temporary Color" by Jackie Greene and Tim Bluhm
"Grindstone" by Jackie Greene and Tim Bluhm
"Messin' With The Kid" by Mel London

Special thanks to my family:
Karen Hamamura, Brian Nelson, Charles Nelson,
Kelly Nelson, Alex Nelson and Tom Gunterman.

With heartfelt gratitude to my friends and teachers:
David Simon-Baker, Tim Bluhm, Steve Berlin and Phil Lesh.

ABOUT THE AUTHOR

Jackie Greene was born in Salinas, California. As a child, he learned to play the guitar and piano. He continues to write songs, compose music and tour. He lives in Northern California.

Made in the USA
Charleston, SC
07 June 2011